Egyptian Textiles and British Capital
1930-1956

Robert L. Tignor

THE AMERICAN UNIVERSITY IN CAIRO PRESS

Dar el Kutub No. 2750/88
ISBN 977 424 186 X

Printed in Egypt by The American University in Cairo Press

Contents

Tables

Preface

While in Britain commencing research into the role of business communities in African decolonization, I came upon the records of two important textile firms—Bradford Dyers Association and Calico Printers Association. Both companies had investments in the Egyptian textile sector stretching back into the 1930s, and these records, consisting of board minutes, reports, and letters, were so extensive and interesting that they seemed to warrant close attention. Of particular value were an extraordinary series of letters by board members written from Egypt during the 1930s in anticipation of an eventual British investment there. These gave a comprehensive portrait of the textile sector and its prospects for development at the moment when a concerted development effort was beginning.

The records shed light on two distinct and significant questions. First, they illuminate the whole evolution of Egypt's textile industry, central to the development effort in that country following the tariff reform of 1930. Bradford and Calico created joint ventures with Egypt's two most powerful indigenous firms: Filature Nationale d'Égypte and the Misr Spinning and Weaving Company. While the Bradford and Calico board records are not so full as they would have been had the parent firms exercised a closer surveillance over their local affiliates, they do provide a fuller account of the progression of this industry than any materials previously available to scholars.

Second, the records are full of insight into questions of direct foreign investment in developing countries. The inaccessibility of business records has hampered work in this field. Consequently scholars have sought to answer the hotly debated questions of why investment was undertaken and what was its impact in host countries, without being able to go directly to the reports and minutes of the business concerns themselves. The Calico and Bradford records offer answers to such compelling questions as how and why the original investment decisions were made, who favored investment and who opposed, what development vision, if any, informed the early decision to invest, and how well, at least in the minds of the metropolitan directors, the investment lived up to its original projections.

What proved to be the most unexpected finding of this study was the power of the periphery—the influence of local businessmen, even at the expense of metropolitan concerns. Of course, in the political history of the Third World local factors and local actors have achieved recognition. Rarely, however, has it been suggested that within far-flung business organizations and multinational enterprises businessmen on the spot have been able to assert their interests over the metropole. This case study, though admittedly of only two firms representing a declining metropolitan industry, forces us to reconsider these assumptions. At virtually every stage indigenous businessmen and politicians had a say in Calico and Bradford involvement in Egypt—whether to enter, how much to invest, when and how to expand, and how, as the investment declined, to withdraw. It was fitting that Bradford and Calico lost authority to local managers and were finally unable to prevent the development they most feared—the nationalization of their enterprises.

My surprise at the Bradford-Calico story led me in turn to question the typicality of their experience. Was the autonomy enjoyed by local textile operatives an aberration? Did other firms operating in Egypt have similar experiences? This query led to a general consideration of the position of foreign capital in Egypt—the elements of overseas control and domination and the degree of local initiative—on the eve of the Egyptian takeover of most foreign assets in 1956. This inquiry serves as a final and concluding chapter to this study.

In the course of carrying out this work I have incurred numerous debts—intellectual as well as personal. The first are to the guardians of the business records themselves. I should like to thank Harry Leach of Tootals for allowing me to see the Calico records, even those materials not yet turned over to the Manchester Central Library but located in one of Tootal's workshops, awaiting delivery to the library. At Bradford Dyers, Jim Allison and Duncan Fisher were unfailingly helpful. They imparted their own considerable knowledge of Beida Dyers to me. Mr. Allison made available in his home a set of Bradford records relating to the firm's Egyptian enterprise. Both men read and commented on a draft of this work and made vital corrections and suggestions. I need hardly add—but should in order to spare them any concern—that while the final product owes much to them, any factual mistakes or errors in interpretation are my own.

The work also benefited from the advice of fellow scholars who read the original draft and offered suggestions. I would be remiss if I did not thank Henry Bienen, Mark Gersovitz, Arno Mayer, Stanley Stein, John Waterbury, and Mira Wilkins. At the same time I would again remind readers that the deficiencies in this study are mine.

The clerical staff of the History Department of Princeton University must surely be relieved to see this manuscript completed. They worked patiently on tables and dealt with a stubborn computer with good cheer. I owe thanks to Doris Gardner, Kari Hoover, Robin Huffman, and Pamela Long.

1
Introduction

Multinational corporations may well be the most powerful economic actors of the twentieth century. Their economic and political prowess are thought to be so awesome that most governments, particularly those in the Third World, lack the resources to rein them in. Among scholars, the power and reach of these conglomerates are emphasized by dependency theorists like Andre Gunder Frank and Samir Amin, who hold that they retard progress in the Third World, as well as by those who contend the opposite.

The multinational experience has been more varied than most scholars indicate. To this day studies have focused on the great conglomerates, those arising out of the most dynamic industrial sectors and countries, and they have overlooked declining metropolitan countries and industries. The Imperial Chemical Industries, Unilever, and the oil companies are not the only multinationals. Many firms qualifying to be considered multinationals by regularly accepted definitions do not have vast human and financial resources. Nor are they in a position to exercise influence easily and effectively at long distances from their metropoles. At their home offices they lack information about local political, social, and economic conditions, and their ability to sway local elites is limited. Numerous smaller multinationals aspire to the kind of economic suzerainty enjoyed by the greater companies, but they rarely achieve such hegemony.

This study explores the history of two such aspiring multinationals: Calico Printers Association and Bradford Dyers Association, textile firms based in the English North. In the late 1920s their financial decline at home and loss of export markets abroad drove them to search for new economic opportunities in the rest of the world. One of their investment areas was Egypt where they created joint ventures. Formerly Egypt had been a major export market for them. Although neither firm became a great multinational corporation, both would be considered multinational according to generally accepted scholarly definitions in vogue today. They created overseas affiliates in different parts of the world, and they placed large portions of their financial resources outside the metropole. Yet as this study will argue, they did not exercise the kind of control over their local affiliates or the general influence in the local economy which most scholarly works on multinationals assume.

A set of extraordinary records, made available by executives of Bradford Dyers and Calico Printers, have made it possible to examine the activities of these firms in Egypt.[1] The records themselves constitute a rare catalogue of information concerning business decisions and the development of an important industry in a Third World country. They consist of detailed and illuminating letters written by British textile directors from Egypt, describing economic conditions there and offering advice about investment opportunities. They also include board minutes and the reports and documents laid before the board prior to discussions.

The first purpose of this study is to trace the evolution of the textile industry in Egypt; a second concern is to evaluate the contribution of foreign capital to the Egyptian effort to industrialize and bring economic betterment to its population. From the 1930s, when these firms first invested in Egyptian plants, until their expropriation following the British-French-Israeli invasion of 1956 these two parent companies were intimately involved in all aspects of Egyptian textile development. The second concern—evaluating the impact of foreign capital on the Egyptian development process—will be consciously framed in terms of the ongoing and intense debate concerning the effect of direct foreign investment on developing countries.

While there is disconcertingly little scholarly consensus about the influence of multinational corporations in the Third World, most of the main questions of this debate are clear. These issues constitute a focus of attention in this study. The debate itself divides clearly albeit roughly between the dependency theorists who attribute harmful effects to multinationals and the liberal or mainstream social scientists who value the economic, social, and technological contributions multinationals make to the Third World.

A multinational is here defined as any large-scale firm of the developed nations having branches and subsidiaries located around the world. Multinationals are to be distinguised from international firms, which are exclusively concerned with the sale of products manufactured at home and thus have only distribution and selling agencies abroad.[2] They are also to be distinguished from firms having portfolio, as distinct from direct, investment in overseas companies. The holding of a minority of the stock instruments in another firm (usually taken to be less than 10 percent) does not ensure management control, and management authority is an essential feature of a multinational business empire. Although a few multinationals specialize in a single economic activity, most have expanded their economic functions, using the headquarters for corporate coordination and control. Multinationals are also characterized by the large size of their financial resources, although it would be fruitless to try to establish any financial cutoff point. Many have oligopolistic market control; certainly all aspire to it.[3]

Six crucial questions emerge from the literature on multinationals and their impact on developing countries. They will be addressed throughout this study. They are: 1. the reasons for expansion; 2. the method and terms of entry; 3. the economic consequences; 4. the appropriateness of the technology; 5. the political environment created; and 6. the social and cultural consequences.

1. *Reasons for expansion.* The debate over the expansion of multinationals divides sharply over whether expansion occurs for aggressive or defensive purposes. Many scholars depict large-scale firms as moving inexorably into foreign countries in search of new investment opportunities for excess profits, taking advantage of cheap labor and the prospects of higher profit margins, and gaining more certain control over raw materials and all stages of the manufacturing process.[4] Other scholars, however, drawing largely on the history of the product cycle, contend that overseas involvement is defensive, with firms seeking to protect already-existing markets from local competitors. According to the product cycle theory, a firm develops a new product and takes over domestic and foreign markets. With the passage of time and the diffusion of manufacturing techniques, new firms spring up at home and abroad. The erection of tariff barriers overseas or the abridging of patent processes are often the triggers for decisions to open overseas subsidiaries. In order to defend markets the parent firm is compelled to establish local manufacturing plants.[5]

2. *Terms of entry.* The critics of multinational enterprises aver that the conglomerates, with their vast economic and financial resources and their international prestige, extract exorbitant tax, tariff, and monopolistic concessions when entering a foreign country. These privileges are whittled down only very gradually and grudgingly by means of acrimonious negotiations, often punctuated by actual shows of force.

The defenders of multinationals claim that Third World bureaucrats, trained in European and American business schools, know precisely the terms needed to attract vital foreign investment. They drive shrewd and successful bargains. Moreover, for all the charters and treaties of entry which yield lucrative returns to foreign investors, numerous other ventures prove unsuccessful and force the foreign businessman to accept losses. Once financial gains are realized, host-country bureaucrats, armed with the threat of nationalization and supported by popular nationalist sentiment, revise the original concessions, paring down the profits accruing to the foreigner and increasing the monies paid over to the host country.[6]

3. *Economic consequences.* The economic effects of direct foreign investment are the core of the debate on multinationals, which has generated a vast literature. The first studies appeared in the 1950s as Asian and African states moved toward independence. These works extolled the benefits of foreign corporations, believing that they could supply much-needed capital and technical and managerial talent. In the influential *Report on Industrialization and the Gold Coast* (1953), W. Arthur Lewis, the Manchester-based economist, argued that no unalterable differences existed between foreign and domestic capital. Both sought high returns on capital and reinvested surplus profits. Eschewing state-run factories in a country which desperately required state expenditure on public services and infrastructure, Lewis believed that an industrial growth rate of 5 percent per year could be achieved through an alliance of foreign enterprise with the state and African businesses.

Later, a set of counterarguments took shape, stressing the harmful effects of foreign capital. The first criticisms were offered even during the decade of optimism, the 1950s. The early reservations (Myrdal on the backwash effects of capital and Singer in his studies on the unequal gains to investing and host countries) eventually crystallized into a perspective on backwardness and underdevelopment.[7] By the late 1970s and 1980s dependency had come to the fore; mainstreamers were on the defensive.

Critics have insisted that far from supplying capital and managerial talent, multinationals absorbed what little capital and managerial capability existed in the host society, thereby preventing indigenous industrialization. Additionally, through the excessive profits they repatriated, these firms enhanced the wealth of Europe and North America at the expense of the developing societies.

In their writings on dependency, Baran, Frank, and Amin leave one with the inescapable impression that the Western intrusion impoverished the Third World. Following this line, Colin Leys showed that Western firms in Kenya repatriated £80 million more capital than they brought into the country between 1964 and 1970.[8] The favored instrument for draining large amounts of capital out of the Third World, even in the face of watchful Third World bureaucracies, was transfer pricing. By fixing the prices of products sold among their subsidiaries, conglomerates brought capital from the periphery to the center.

More recently writers have presented a more subtle view of the economic consequences of multinationals, elaborating concepts like associated dependent development. Although there is less consensus among the dependency writers of the 1970s and 1980s, certain themes continue to dominate the literature. First, while many of the dependency critics concede that multinationals promote economic growth and even structural economic change, they stress the deleterious consequences of multinational exposure. In particular the ties of economic and political subordination remain. In many areas foreign firms promote enclave development, creating rich and privileged groups of managers and skilled workers who live at standards far above the rest of society and arouse jealousies. More importantly, the multinationals strengthen the international division of labor by linking a superexploited economic periphery with a superwealthy Western world. Dependent development occurs under the aegis of multinational business firms; the income gaps between north and south grow wider, based as they are on unequal exchange.

4. *Inappropriate technology.* According to the critics, one of the reasons for the baleful economic consequences of multinationals is that they introduce technologies inappropriate to the Third World. Conglomerates export manufacturing techniques developed in the capital-rich and labor-scarce West and produce in Asia and Africa the wrong mix of factor proportions. Their capital-intensive industrial plants provide little employment and intensify economic inequalities.

The defenders argue that the multinationals, far from misunderstanding the factor proportions, are more likely than local firms to respond to variations in the costs of labor and capital. They do, in fact, possess a wider experience than local firms. They conduct more research in the adaptation of manufacturing techniques on the periphery than do local firms. Local manufacturers tend slavishly to imitate Western models. Research into appropriate manufacturing technologies, it is argued, should not in fact be a primary responsibility of corporations. It should be carried out by the host state and universities, but political instability and the lack of commitment to economic growth stymie such programs.[9]

5. *Political environment.* While political and cultural impacts are more nebulous matters, they bulk large in the controversy over direct foreign investment. The liberal mainstreamers argue that multinationals are largely uninvolved in local politics, pleading unfamiliarity with political institutions, or they confine themselves to recognized pressure groups. Critics see multinationals, especially the large and heavily capitalized companies, as veritable states within a state. These firms influence a whole range of

economic decisions vital to their financial well-being (tariffs, taxation, and the like); they also favor conservative and autocratic political institutions and deter the emergence of mass democratic politics. The critics of foreign firms insist that the great corporations have used their alliances with politically conservative groups—the compradors—to undermine liberal and democratic elements.[10]

6. *Cultural consequences.* Critics and apologists agree that economic developments have far-ranging cultural effects. For the critics most of these effects are harmful. They undermine authentic historical traditions in favor of poorly understood Western values. Advertising is held to be the most pernicious weapon employed by multinationals in their cultural assault. Steven Langdon claims that in Kenya foreign corporations used advertising barrages and played upon status themes and the superiority of Western ways to destroy the indigenous shoe and soap manufacturing establishments.[11] The defenders counter that the role of advertising has been greatly exaggerated and that if Asian and African consumers prefer products made by multinationals it is because these goods have clear and compelling advantages and bring improvements in the quality of life.[12]

These six areas of inquiry provide the framework for this investigation into the textile industry in Egypt and the British financial and technical contributions to it. Did the foreign firms enter Egypt largely for defensive or offensive reasons? Were they able to secure privileged positions within the Egyptian economy? Did they bring a technology well adapted to the capital and labor proportions of Egypt? What social, political, and cultural impact did they have?

The time frame of this study—1930 to 1956—is bounded by important international events. Egypt's modern textile industry did not emerge until the Egyptian government enacted tariff reform in 1930. From that year until the British-French-Israeli invasion of 1956 foreign investment played a key role in the evolution of this crucial industry. Of the foreign groups with an interest in Egyptian textiles, English firms predominated. In the 1930s Bradford Dyers, Bleachers Association, and Calico Printers linked up with two local firms—Filature Nationale d'Égypte and the Misr Spinning and Weaving Company—to establish new and technically sophisticated firms in Egypt.

While the story of British investment is a complex one, it does offer some clear answers to the major questions concerning foreign investment. To preview the main lines of the argument, the British firms entered Egypt defensively, seeking to retain a once lucrative but now diminishing market. The main agents of British investment were not, however, the British textile men themselves, but their local Egyptian distributors on whom the metropolitan firms had always relied for local market information. The terms of entry of the firms were far from privileged. Although at first contemplating the establishment of independent companies, tightly controlled from Britain, the British executives were forced to the conclusion that Egypt was too strange and in many ways hostile a political and economic environment for independent action. They opted to join with local firms and powerful local entrepreneurs. With the passage of time (and despite large amounts of capital tied up in their Egyptian enterprises) they allowed managerial control to slip into the hands of men on the spot.

One of the reasons that these firms were unable to establish better entry terms and become more powerful forces within the Egyptian political economy was their own declining position at home. Bradford and Calico lacked the requisite financial, technical, and managerial resources to dominate Egyptian textiles. They were forced into subordinate positions even within their own joint ventures.

Even so, the British companies brought an industrial technology ideally suited to Egypt's evolving textile sector. By manufacturing a product superior to that which was produced in the country, the new firms lifted Egypt to a higher stage of textile development. Their specialized and efficient finishing, dyeing, and bleaching techniques were greatly needed, and their plants were organized to take advantage of Egypt's different capital and labor factor proportions. Although the firms rewarded themselves with handsome dividends, they also plowed a large proportion of their profits back into the country, spurring the country's textile expansion during and after World War II.

The political and cultural impacts are more difficult to judge. On their own the firms had little political clout. Hence they were compelled to work in league with recognized pressure groups, notably the British Chamber of Commerce and the Egyptian Federation of Industry. Their record of influence was one of only modest success. While they enjoyed government favor in the form of tariff protection, they also feared the populist nationalism of the state. Their worst fears were confirmed by the nationalization legislation of 1956 and 1957.

As for the contribution of British textile investment to Egyptian industrialization, it is difficult to argue that the textile sector was a powerful engine of economic change. The textile firms—Egyptian and joint ventures alike—were grossly inefficient, worked at excess capacity, and produced more than the local population could afford to purchase. In part the failure occurred because these companies operated behind protective tariff barriers and were not forced to be highly efficient. But equally important, especially for the foreign firms, which tended to be more efficient than the local plants, Egypt's textile plants used expensive, long-staple Egyptian cotton. A powerful agricultural lobby stymied industry efforts to import cheap cotton and thus rendered impossible the effort to put the local industry on an international standard.

The conventional wisdom about multinationals is that whether they are seen to do good or ill in local economies, they are forceful and disciplined entities. The evidence from these British overseas enterprises suggests, however, that this perception of economic rationality and centralized coordination does not hold true for all cases. Like so much else this stereotype is based on the behavior of the successful giants. Smaller, less powerful conglomerates are often unable to mobilize substantial managerial, financial, and political resources or to project their influence in a host country. If the Calico and Bradford stories have validity, what indeed seems to count is the integration of overseas affiliates into a single corporate empire so that the wishes of the center can be translated into actions at the periphery. This kind of control requires the flow of information from the affiliate to the home office and the posting of capable and energetic managers to the affiliate—men on the rise who will make their first mark overseas, rather than men on the decline who are serving out the final stages of their business careers.

Background to the Egyptian Textile Industry

Curiously the emergence of a modern textile industry was long delayed in Egypt. Following Muhammad Ali's precocious and aborted industrialization in the first half of the nineteenth century, no sustained effort at industrializing occurred until after tariff reform was achieved. In contrast India, China, Japan, and numerous countries in Latin America had long before embarked on industrial schemes and had created modern textile industries. Late industrialization left its mark on Egypt's economic development. The textile industries when they appeared were few and heavily capitalized. Integrated with one another through common board members, they were also highly dependent on the state for supports.

A partial explanation for this arrested development was the way Egypt fitted into the international economy. From the 1840s onwards Egypt was a free trade area. The country's 8 percent *ad valorem* tariff on imports did not keep goods out, and the policies of Egypt's rulers—its Khedives until 1882 and afterwards the British overlords of the country—promoted the cultivation and export of cotton and the import of European manufactures.

From the outset, textiles were the major component of Egypt's import trade. They constituted about one third of the value of Egyptian imports during the 1880s and 1890s, and between 25 and 30 percent between 1905 and the outbreak of World War I. Britain was Egypt's chief textile supplier, accounting for roughly 60 percent of the value of Egypt's textile imports between 1903 and 1913.[13]

Set as firmly as it was in the colonial economic orbit, the country did not develop the institutional and infrastructural framework needed for rapid industrial growth. The population was accustomed to foreign products and would have spurned local goods for the heavily advertised imported commodities. The state offered neither tariff protection (where international treaties forbade change until 1930), nor favorable railway rates, which discriminated against the industrial sector and in favor of agriculture. It maintained excise duties on locally manufactured products, and the country lacked a well developed capital market by which risk capital could be mobilized for new enterprises. Even had these problems been overcome, the country was without a coterie of entrepreneurs prepared to launch industrial companies and schemes.

Another reason why a modern textile industry was slow to emerge was the continuing viability and even vitality of Egypt's artisanal spinning and weaving industry. The structure of this industry had not changed greatly during the nineteenth century despite the influx of European textiles. M.P.S. Girard, one of Napoleon's savants, found the Egyptian textile industry in 1800 thriving and regionally specialized. Upper Egypt was the center for cotton spinning and weaving, exploiting its access to the most valued cotton, grown around Esna. Weavers from the area supplemented these supplies with cotton imported from Syria. In Fayoum and the Delta, linen was the dominant material. Silk, brought from Syria, was woven in Damietta, Mahalla, and Cairo, and was used mainly for luxury furnishings in the homes of the well-to-do. Weaving was a specialized, male occupation; women did most of the spinning in their homes. Wool cloth, Egypt's most widely produced textile, was woven in virtually all villages and worn by the peasantry.[14]

Three separate sets of reports, produced between 1910 and 1925, demonstrated that the local textile handicraft industry had changed little over the course of a century. Regional specialization still existed. Mahalla and Damietta continued to lead in silk production, and Cairo served as the major *entrepôt* for dyes and looms. The most significant changes included an increase in cotton spinning and weaving, as cotton had replaced wool as the preferred textile, no doubt a reflection of the massive expansion in the cultivation of cotton in Egypt during the nineteenth century. More and more Egyptian weavers had come to rely on imported rather than locally spun yarn.[15]

Sidney Wells, Director of Agricultural, Industrial, and Commercial Education in Egypt, wrote the first of the three reports, publishing it in *Égypte contemporaine*.[16] Based on Wells's analyses of the census returns of 1897 and 1907 and detailed reports from inspectors for the provinces of Qalyubia, Fayoum, and Daqahlia, the document found weaving still to be a thriving handicraft industry. Mahalla retained its prominence for silk products while Akhmim had emerged as a cotton-manufacturing locale, called by some the Manchester of Egypt. In Qalyubia, Wells estimated that an ordinary village of 300 inhabitants was likely to have fifteen to twenty looms; one loom to a house, although a few places had two or three looms. The provincial capital—Qalyub—was a textile center, possessing workshops with thirty looms and selling finished textiles in Cairo and to neighboring Arab tribesmen. The weaving machines employed in these various centers were simple ones, locally made. Most had only two warps, operated by pedals. At Qalyub, however, the more sophisticated machines had four to six pedals, and many were brought from Cairo.

The inhabitants of Fayoum province had carried specialization to a higher degree. Numerous villages had no weaving at all and traded with those communities where the weavers were concentrated. The village of Fidimin, fourteen kilometers from Madinat al-Fayoum, not only served the entire province, but exported its surplus garments as far as Tanta, Alexandria, and Syria. Damietta was still a hub for silk production. It boasted no fewer than forty workshops, some with only two or three looms, others with many more. The total number of looms in the city was 200. The largest workshop belonged to 'Abd al-Fattah al-Lawzi, scion of a family which had for many decades dominated silk weaving in the city. His factory contained thirty-seven looms and produced about 170,000 square meters of silk per year, accounting for one third of the city's production. Damietta silk was mainly woven into black garments worn by Egyptian women.

The report of the Egyptian Commission on Commerce and Industry, published in 1918, confirmed Wells's findings.[17] If anything, it demonstrated that the war had forced Egyptian artisans to expand output. The commissioners estimated that there were 2,455 looms at Mahalla, 450 at Akhmim, 390 at Damietta (still specialized in silk but now possessing double the number of looms observed by Wells), 2,000 at Qalyub, and 1,000 at Nakkad in Qena province, which exported its piece goods to the Sudan. While most of the sophisticated dyeing was done in Cairo, Mahalla,

Damietta, and Qalyub, nearly every village did some dyeing of cloth.

After the war the newly created Ministry of Commerce and Industry sent out inspectors to report on local industries.[18] Their reports constitute the third comprehensive portrait of Egypt's artisanal sector. The inspectorate estimated that Egypt had as many as 13,000 hand looms and produced 22,000,000 square meters of cloth per year. Egyptian weavers continued their dependence on imported yarns; only about 4,000,000 kilograms of yarn were spun locally, worth LE 1,000,000, far from enough for the local weaving industry.

Although much of the spinning and weaving was done on a very localized basis, a few skilled workmen were set off from the rank and file. Their finished products, always in great demand, were displayed at the various industrial exhibitions, which the Egyptian business community organized from the beginning of the twentieth century onwards. During the 1926 industrial exhibition, for instance, the reporter of *Égypte industrielle*, organ of the Egyptian Federation of Industries, heaped praise on two silk manufacturers, 'Abd al-Fattah al-Lawzi from Damietta and 'Abd al-Ghani Salim 'Abduh. Lawzi was considered to have a better future because of his commitment to modern machines. His sons had received a technical education in silk weaving in France. 'Abduh, on the other hand, worked in the traditional mode. Both businessmen produced cloth with oriental motifs. Other smaller, but nonetheless highly regarded artisans were 'Abd al-Hamid Mahir and 'Abd al-Razik Hilmi, both of whom had graduated from the School of Weaving at Abu Tig. They were esteemed for their foulards, bedcovers, tablecloths, and shawls. Shaykh Muhammad al-Sa'id Barakat from the famed textile metropolis of al-Mahalla al-Kubra, produced widely sought-after woolens.[19] Even as late as 1930, just prior to the erection of protective tariffs, the Egyptian Department of Commerce and Industry estimated that the country had twenty thousand hand looms, capable of turning out thirty million square meters of cotton, artificial silk, linen, and woolen piece cloths.[20] Nonetheless, Egypt's textile artisans were ultimately doomed by the cheap Japanese, Italian, and Indian textile imports in the 1930s and a rising local modern industry.

A small modern textile industry had come into existence at the end of the nineteenth century; its presence was of crucial importance for the later evolution of the industry. In the late 1890s a brief financial flourishing (more a speculative bubble than a concerted economic expansion) saw the creation of a number of new joint stock companies. Among these companies were two aspiring modern textile firms, both administered by foreign businessmen resident in Egypt: Anglo-Egyptian Spinning and Weaving Company and

Egyptian Cotton Mills. Neither proved viable. Lord Cromer, Britain's consul-general in the country and virtual ruler, enacted an 8 percent excise tax on local manufactures (equivalent to the import duty on all products), thereby signalling to these businessmen that the government would not encourage their efforts. The speculative bubble burst in the crash of 1907 taking most of these new companies with it. The Cotton Mills firm failed outright, but the Anglo-Egyptian Cotton and Spinning Company managed to sell its assets, originally valued at £150,000, to a new group of foreign residential investors and managers for £37,500.[21] The new owners reorganized the firm under a new name, la Filature Nationale d'Égypte. Filature was to play a decisive role in subsequent Egyptian textile industrialization, led by Linus Gasche, its Swiss-born, Italian-trained, and Egyptian-domiciled director.

Filature came into being because its predecessor, unlike many of the other new companies created primarily to take advantage of the speculative mania, had actually purchased equipment and acquired land for a plant near Alexandria. The company would have failed had it not been for World War I. Cut off from traditional European suppliers, Egyptian consumers turned to local manufacturers. By 1918 the firm had 20,000 spindles, 560 looms, and its own power plant of 1,000 horsepower, with a back-up unit of 650 horsepower.[22] The wartime profits were so substantial that the firm was able to make a free distribution to its shareholders of two new shares for every share already held, thereby raising the number of shares in the company from 12,500 to 37,500 and the total nominal equity from LE 50,000 to LE 150,000. In the same year that the firm made this munificent distribution of shares, it also paid a dividend of 117 piasters per share (or 28.5 percent of nominal capital).[23]

But Filature's economic well-being was highly artificial. By war's end the company, relatively heavily capitalized by Egyptian standards, manufactured only coarse and roughly woven gray cloth. Its technical capacities were limited, and its output was far from competitive in price or quality with the standard imports from Britain and India, not to mention the new, cheaper, and very colorful Japanese and Italian imports, which were beginning to flood into Egypt. Indeed, the state had helped Filature to survive by removing the excise on its manufactures between 1909 and 1918. It then reintroduced the excise tax but at a reduced rate of 4 percent. This tax, coupled with the huge influx of foreign textiles, proved a great burden for the company, and in 1925 the state once again abolished the excise. Still the company's finances were precarious.[24]

During the war Filature had 900 employees and produced nine million square meters of cotton piece goods per year.[25] By 1922 the factory had increased its work force to 1,500 employees and had 40,000 spindles, using Egyptian cotton of lower grades. Its annual output was 4.25 million pounds of yarn and nine million yards of gray sheeting cloth.[26] By 1930 on the eve of tariff reform Filature had increased its plant capacity to 60,000 spindles and 800 power looms. Yet its production had declined, for the factory used 60,000 *qantars* of cotton to manufacture 3.5 million pounds of cotton yarn and six million yards of gray calico and damor fabrics.[27] No doubt the decline in output reflected the company's inability to compete with textile imports. Its financial results were equally disappointing. Its dividends had fallen sharply from their high point in 1919-20 (LE 2.53 per share of LE 4 per value) to 19.5 piasters in 1922-23. The dividend on ordinary shares was eliminated completely in fiscal year 1927-28, while dividends on preference shares, newly issued at 6.5 percent in 1926, were paid only for the first two years (1925-26 and 1926-27) and then were allowed to go into arrears until 1932-33. Meanwhile the reserve funds declined from LE 84,154 in 1922-23 to LE 61,629 on the eve of tariff reform.[28]

The presence of a heavily capitalized, inefficient, yet politically influential firm established in many ways the costs of entry into this important industrial sector. Filature was vertically integrated; it spun and wove cotton and had small bleaching, dyeing, and printing works. While more specialized non-integrated modern firms might have come into existence, Filature's presence made other entrepreneurs hesitate. Integrated firms had some marked advantages, but these should not be exaggerated. Economies of scale existed, although a well-run firm specializing in one of the three textile branches (spinning, weaving, and finishing) need not fear the large plants on purely economic grounds. An integrated firm would have lower delivery and sale costs as the product moved from one stage of the manufacturing process to the next.[29] The one other modern textile establishment, the silk factory of the Lawzi family at Damietta, although on a much smaller scale (capitalization of LE 24,000), also aspired to vertical integration. Already it spun and wove silk and had plans to create finishing works. Thus, the only area wide open for small specialized firms was the apparel stage—the preparation of cloth for wearing.

Another factor worked to favor domination by a few, heavily capitalized, vertically integrated, and politically powerful firms: the fact that tariff reform was scheduled to come into being at a precise time, 1930. The leading business magnates endeavored to get a jump on their competitors by establishing large and powerful firms in the late 1920s and thus make it difficult for new firms to enter the textile arena.

In anticipation of tariff reform, Filature expanded its capital and purchased more machines. In 1926 it issued 18,750 preference shares at 6.5 percent (LE 4 per share), thus increasing its nominal equity capital from LE 150,000 to LE 225,000. In the following year it increased its preference shares capitalization to LE 320,000, which made Filature the sixth most heavily capitalized industrial company in the country. Preference shares were issued rather than ordinary shares so that substantial funds could be raised and the company would have financial elasticity at a time of rapid plant expansion.[30] The high interest rate attached to the preference shares (6.5 percent) almost proved to be the company's undoing in the 1930s; they had to be bought up in a desperate effort to save the company's finances.

One business conglomerate which was quite willing, even eager, to pay these rising entry costs was Tal'at Harb's Bank Misr. When Tal'at Harb founded the bank in 1920, he envisaged it as a force for economic diversification and industrialization. His investigative trip to Germany before 1914 persuaded him that banks could spearhead new business and economic endeavors. It also convinced him that cartels could ensure the efficient allocation of scarce economic resources.[31] Although the bank's first business ventures were on a decidedly small scale, Tal'at Harb regarded textiles as the linchpin of any industrial effort. Even as early as 1923 and 1924 in speeches at al-Mahalla al-Kubra, destined to be the center of the bank's textile effort, Tal'at Harb praised the city for maintaining a good balance between industry and agriculture and spoke of his aspiration to build upon Mahalla's textile tradition.[32]

Tal'at Harb's first big industrial venture, the Misr Spinning and Weaving Company, began with a large capitalization of LE 300,000, which put the company at once on a financial par with Filature. It did not remain at this level for long. Its directors increased the equity capital to LE 500,000 in 1933, LE 800,000 in 1934, and LE 1 million in 1936, in keeping with their intention to establish a vertically integrated spinning and weaving works at al-Mahalla al-Kubra and to transform this Egyptian Delta city into the textile capital of the Near East.[33] The Misr Spinning and Weaving Company was by far the most heavily capitalized Misr industrial venture. By 1936 its equity capital equaled that of the bank itself.

Tal'at Harb was delighted at the enthusiastic public response to the new Misr Spinning and Weaving Company. He could in fact have raised the entire capital through public subscription, but preferred to keep tight control over the new firm.[34] Accordingly, while he brought in a larger group of original investors than he did for the other Misr industrial ventures (thirty-four in all, almost all of whom were large landowners), he reserved 45 percent of the share capital for Bank Misr itself, another 33 percent for two Misr affiliated companies, and 8 percent for individuals like himself who were sitting at that time on the board of the bank.[35] The connection between the bank and the Misr Spinning and Weaving Company was cemented in this way.

The local financial press welcomed these heavily capitalized firms. Their size and economic power, they argued, would prevent foreign textile concerns from entering Egypt and competing with indigenous industries.[36] Their existence did, in fact, render it difficult for foreign firms to enter Egypt on their own. Nonetheless, their presence, particularly that of the Misr Spinning and Weaving Company with its close ties with government officials and its popularity as an organ of Egyptian national development, also made it difficult for local competitors to arise. Only after World War II did new local firms appear, although even then many of the new companies made arrangements with the two textile giants.

Thus, even in the 1920s Egypt's modern textile firms had been set firmly on the path of large capitalization, concentration, and vertical integration. This tendency had occurred in spite of the fact that economies of scale were not involved, and equally, more labor-intensive plants might have suited Egypt's capital/labor factor proportions. The reasons are not hard to discern: the small number of genuine entrepreneurs; the inhospitality of banks to small-scale businessmen; the emergence of two giants, under state sponsorship; and the long delay in achieving tariff freedom. The tendency toward large size and vertical integration was to be confirmed by the powerful entry of two British textile firms in the 1930s.[37]

Additionally the two giant textile firms had assumed a position of prominence, if not preeminence, in the political economy of interwar Egypt. The Misr Spinning and Weaving Company was the most heavily capitalized company of the expanding Misr complex of companies and thus the flagship of Egypt's industrial effort. By the 1930s even Tal'at Harb's most severe critics conceded that he had won a privileged position for Bank Misr and its affiliated companies among the Egyptian public and influential politicians. The British commercial attaché believed that the Misr companies were destined to survive and even to prosper, if only because Tal'at Harb had succeeded in making his enterprise a national asset and was certain to have essential government supports, whenever and wherever needed.

The two textile conglomerates represented the two major and sometimes competing wings of the nascent local bourgeoisie. The Misr Spinning and Weaving Company was a predominantly Egyptian enterprise; its shareholders and directors were required to be Egyptian nationals. Every effort was made to use Egyptian technicians and managers, although foreign textile experts were engaged. Filature was run by foreign nationals resident in Egypt. Although many of these so-called foreign businessmen came from families who had resided in Egypt for several generations (even in some cases for centuries) they had not acquired Egyptian nationality. Nor during the nineteenth century and the first two decades of the twentieth did they demonstrate much interest in being naturalized, given the tax and judicial privileges which foreigners then enjoyed in Egypt. Later in the 1930s, 40s, and 50s when foreign privileges had been whittled away and some may have contemplated naturalization, the procedures involved were difficult and time-consuming. Few of those from business families became Egyptian nationals. These individuals emerged out of the still substantial, prosperous, well-educated, and well-connected foreign community residing in Egypt. Originally they had been involved in financing the cotton crop and selling European manufactures in Egypt. But men like Linus Gasche of Filature and Henri Naus of the Egyptian Sugar Company pioneered the industrialization and diversification of the Egyptian economy. They had decided advantages over the Egyptian entrepreneurs, not merely because they enjoyed the privileges accorded to all foreigners living in Egypt under the Capitulations (trial in the mixed courts or consular courts, no taxation without the approval of their national governments, and virtual inviolability of domicile), but also because they were able to attract overseas capital and talent more easily than the indigenous firms.

By 1930, on the eve of Egyptian tariff reform, textiles occupied an important place in Egypt's import substitution strategy. The numerous reports counseling industrialization—from the influential *Report of the Commission on Commerce and Industry* of 1916 to the documents issued by the local financial press, pressure groups, and the various government ministries and committees—all stressed textile development. Moreover the two local textile firms were well represented on Egypt's pressure groups. Tal'at Harb and Linus Gasche were members of the influential Egyptian Federation of Industries, and Tal'at Harb's Misr Spinning and Weaving Company board included many political notables. Thus the industrialists were confident that the government would encourage textiles through tariffs, taxation policy, and general programs of encouragement.

Egypt's parliamentary system, established in the aftermath of World War I, also favored the rising industries. All the political parties of the interwar era—the majoritarian Wafdists and the various minority parties which held office frequently—espoused the strategy of import substitution industrialization. The textile industrialists had easy access to the parliament and to the leading ministers, the more so when individuals like Isma'il Sidqi with their close connections to the business world held high office. Sidqi, in fact, was prime minister during the 1930s and then again after World War II.

Nonetheless, the industrialists counted for much less in Egyptian politics than the large landowners, who dominated parliament and Egyptian ministerial offices. When the interest of these two groups clashed, as they did after World War II, the agricultural wing had the upper hand. The industrialists held second rank in the political economy; they had to put forward programs which appealed to the self-interest of the large landowners.

2

British Financial Intervention
in Egyptian Textiles

The British textile sector was an industry in severe decline, set within an economy which was losing its international competitiveness to the rest of Europe and North America. One cannot understand the behavior of the textile executives in Egypt—the risks they took and the mistreatment they received at the hands of their Egyptian affiliates—without being mindful of the deep economic crisis afflicting the British economy during the interwar years. The general British economic statistics are too well known to bear repeating, but some data on the textile industry are in order.

During the twentieth century British industry was losing its world-wide domination over textile production and trade, a domination which in the first half of the nineteenth century had seen British textile exports account for 51 percent of the value of all British exports. During this earlier era British firms owned 60 percent of the world's spindles and 53 percent of its power looms.[1] The decline did not set in until after World War I. Up to the outbreak of World War I British textiles continued to increase in output in home and foreign markets. At that time textiles constituted one quarter of the value of all British exports, and Britain alone exported 70 percent of the volume of cotton piece goods entering into world trade. On the eve of the war the British cotton industry was larger in every respect than at any previous period in its history.[2]

But British industrialists were not able to maintain their international lead in the interwar years. By 1921 the yardage of textiles exported from Britain was less by two thirds than it had been in 1910–1913. The 1920s and 1930s, according to one authority, was a period "of depressed demand and low or nonexistent profits at least after 1921." In 1930 the average capacity utilization in British cotton textile factories was down to 58 percent in spinning and 54 percent in weaving.[3]

The decisions of the British textile executives to open factories in Egypt were taken only after intensive and searching discussions. The records of these discussions and the entire decision-making process provide an opportunity to explore in detail the terms of entry of these corporations. On the surface the decisions seem to conform ideally with the product cycle theory (see p. 3): a metropolitan industry responding in a defensive way, to retain a position in a vital overseas market. No doubt the executives hoped to realize large profits in Egypt (and in other parts of the world where they were soon engaged in similar investments) and anticipated a new spurt of profitability and rising production in these ventures.

A close reading of board minutes and the letters written from Egypt uncovers some unexpected results, however. In the first place the decisions to invest were not the orderly and calculated defensive reactions portrayed in most scholarly studies. They were in many ways desperate, last-ditch efforts to stem precipitous financial declines. They were taken in great haste and with considerable financial risk. Second, much of the initiative came from the periphery rather than the metropole. Local Egyptian merchants, the distributors of British textiles, were at first the moving force, importuning their metropolitan manufacturers to arrest a declining market by investing in Egypt's textile industrialization. Later, Egyptian industrialists in the Misr empire sought an alliance with a European firm. Using their connections with the British Embassy and foreign businessmen, Tal'at Harb and his associates compelled the Bradford group to join with them rather than to set up an independent enterprise in Egypt.

The trigger for Lancashire's intervention in Egyptian textiles was the government's determination to raise tariffs on imported textiles, following the achievement of tariff freedom in 1930. Although the new tariffs were a modest 15 percent at first, they hit a struggling British textile industry hard. Egypt had been a major trading area for Britain in the nineteenth century. Egyptian consumers had placed great value on British-made commodities, particularly textiles. In 1913, for example, 30 percent of all Egyptian imports by value were British and 43 percent of Egyptian exports, mainly cotton of course, were purchased by the British. Indeed, in 1913 1.9 percent of all British exports went to Egypt and 2.1 percent of all British imports came from Egypt (see tables 2.1 and 2.2). The main British exports to Egypt in that year, as in previous years, were coal, textiles, and machinery, which constituted 49, 60, and 47 percent respectively of Egyptian imports of these commodities (see table 2.3). Thus, the decline of textile exports to Egypt (from a high point of 70 percent of all textiles in 1919 to 29 percent in 1929) was of great concern to British industrialists. The prospects of further losses in the Egyptian market, looming because of the new tariff barriers and increased Japanese, Indian, and Italian competition, were keenly debated in the board rooms of leading British firms.

The most concerted effort to deal with this challenge came, not from the spinning and weaving branches of the trade (in great decline and administrative disarray by the 1920s and 1930s[4]) but from the finishing sections (bleaching, printing, and dyeing). Their overseas business had been less damaged. Each one of these specialties was dominated by a single firm, still capable of decisive action: Bleachers Association for bleaching; Bradford Dyers Association among the dyers; and Calico Printers Association for printing. Each had substantial trading interests in Egypt, and each would decide to leap over Egyptian tariff barriers and create a joint venture textile enterprise in that country.

These three firms, destined to have a decisive influence on the evolution of Egyptian industrialization, brought their own metropolitan experience to Egypt. Let us then turn to their historical record. All three companies had come into being at the turn of the twentieth century as part of a general merger movement which affected the textile, brewing, iron and steel, cement, wallpaper, and tobacco industries.[5] The goal of the amalgamation schemes was to reduce competition, pare costs, fix prices, and use the limited public company framework to attract new investment from a wider range of potential investors. Although this effort did in fact succeed in creating a number of new limited public companies and thus spearheaded a transition from family firms to limited liability companies, the mergers did not go nearly as far as they did in the United States.

Bradford, Bleachers, and Calico came into being as a result of the merging of a large number of smaller, mainly family-run businesses. The driving force behind the creation of Calico Printers Association was Lennox B. Lee, who took his father's firm, Rossendale Printing Company, into the new amalgam in 1899.[6] The Calico merger brought together forty-six printing firms (of which fourteen were in Scotland), five Glasgow merchants, five Manchester merchants, and three merchant firms with branches in Manchester and Glasgow. The amalgamation gave Calico 830 printing machines, 277,264 spindles, and 6,656 looms, comprising, according to the prospectus of incorporation, 85 percent of the calico printing industry of Great Britain. Calico's strength lay in the diversity of its production. It "catered for every market in the world which was open to English prints."[7]

Nonetheless, the new limited liability company had serious defects. The company was considerably overvalued. The purchase price of the concerns taken over was £8,047,031 while their certified value was £7,693,504. This overvaluation of roughly £400,000 was the price which the firm had to pay to entice individual sellers to dispose of their own companies. Additionally the newly constituted board had at the outset eighty-four directors, designated on the basis of the number of machines which their branches possessed. Out of this "mob of directors" eight individuals were selected to be managing directors, though these could be overruled by the whole board.[8]

Lee transformed this completely unworkable structure by concentrating power in three bodies: a full board of six; an executive of three and seven advisory committees, each with three to five members. Lee himself became head of the firm in 1908, a position which he held until 1947.

Although Lee's goal had been to restore profitability to the printing trade by reducing competition and costs, his results were only partially successful. He did not succeed in forcing all printers to join his new company, the most notable exceptions being United Turkey Red Company, Ltd. (capitalization £1.5 million) and F. Steiner and Company, Ltd. (£925,000). As a result, Calico never controlled more than 58 percent of total productive capacity, far from the 85 percent promised in the prospectus.[9] Profitability was not great; nor were dividends high. The latter were slightly above 2 percent of nominal capital during the first decade of existence (1900–01 to 1909–10). They rose to 4 percent in the next decade and to 8.25 percent in the 1920s[10] (see table 2.4). But the rise was deceiving and was based to a large extent on the operation of a pricing ring, known as the Federation of Calico Printers, in which the Calico Printers Association played a large role.[11] The Calico output declined steadily during these years, falling from 754 million yards of printed goods in 1907 to 368 million yards in 1929.[12] Suffering from a lack of cooperation from its constituent members and much evasion of price and production guidelines, the Federation of Calico Printers lost its capacity to fix prices between 1928 and 1932, when the industry fell on hard financial times.[13]

Just as Lee was the driving force behind Calico, so George Douglas stamped his personality on Bradford Dyers. This limited liability company came into being in 1898 as Douglas brought his father's firm, Edward Ripley and Sons, dyers at Bowling, near Bradford, into the new company.[14] Bradford was less unwieldy than Calico, consisting initially of twenty-two firms in the Bradford piece-dyeing trade, and controlling 90 percent of that trade. It had less capital (£3 million) at the outset, but through expansion and incorporation of other dyeing firms in Yorkshire and further away it became the seventeenth most heavily capitalized manufacturing company in Britain at £4,310,000 by 1905. (Calico stood fifth with a total capitalization of £8,227,000.)[15] Douglas became the sole managing director of Bradford in 1909, a position he held until his retirement in 1945. He also became chairman of the board in 1924. Perhaps because the new company was smaller, more tightly managed, and had greater control over the local market, the firm enjoyed higher dividend rates. Dividends averaged 6.4 percent in the first decade, rising to 12.5 percent in the next ten-year period and to 15.33 percent in the 1920s, plus a 60 percent capitalized bonus distributed after the 1924–25 fiscal year[16] (see table 2.4).

Bleachers Association, destined to play only a small role in Egypt, also came into being following a merger of 53 different firms in 1900.[17] It had a nominal capital of £6,750,000 and was, in 1905, the ninth most heavily capitalized manufacturing company, with a capital of £6,280,000. Its dividends rose steadily from 2.4 percent in the first decade of existence (1900–01 to 1909–10) to 7.5 percent in the 1910s and to 13 percent in the 1920s (see table 2.4).

The British finishing trades suffered less from overseas competition than did the spinning and weaving firms. British cotton finishers specialized in the upper end of the cotton business—the finer cotton and higher counts which continued to sell well in domestic and overseas markets. In lower count and coarse cotton pieces, British textiles were losing out to local firms and to Japanese, Italian, and Indian export competition.[18] But the finishing firms were far from secure financially in the 1930s. Calico Printers was unable to pay a dividend on its ordinary stock between 1929 and 1947.[19] Its output, which averaged 406 million yards per year during the 1920s, declined to 285 million yards per year in the next decade.[20] Bradford Dyers, which had paid out dividends averaging 15 percent of nominal capital during the 1920s, began to omit dividend payments in 1931. It was unable to issue any payments to its preferred shareholders between 1933 and 1940 even while exhausting its various reserve funds.[21] Bleachers also had to suspend dividend payments during the Depression. The financial mauling of all three brought a sharp decline in their financial position among British manufacturing companies. In 1929 Bleachers was in thirtieth position with a book-value capitalization of £6,266,000. Calico, in thirty-eighth position, had a book value of £5,027,000; Bradford's capitalization of £4,670,000 was only good for forty-seventh position.[22]

The leading textile executives had explanations for this crisis, attributing it to cutthroat competition at home, excess industrial capacity, excessive labor costs, an unresponsive state, and high corporate taxes.[23] In particular, George Douglas, chairman of the board of Bradford Dyers, led the campaign for reform, pressing the government and other textile operatives to allow the large and efficient firms to absorb and if necessary put out of business the small companies. In that way excess capacity would be ended. Douglas was certain that British textiles overseas were not competitive with Japanese products, given the undervalued Japanese yen and the low labor costs in Japan. But he believed that the cartelization of British industry could restore productivity and profitability at home. "The progressive elements in each industry," he asserted, "[should] overcome the obstruction of small minorities to schemes of reorganization which a substantial majority approved as likely to be of advantage to the industry as a whole."[24] Abroad, he favored quota agreements and imperial preference. The efforts at domestic concentration and imperial preference were not notably successful, however. The finishing trades of the textile industry continued their decline throughout the 1930s.

The Calico-Filature Affiliation

The first of the British firms to take an active interest in Egypt was the Calico Printers Association. Their early involvement was predictable, given the fact that they were the most heavily capitalized of the British textile firms and more vertically integrated than their domestic competitors. They did some weaving as well as printing. In addition, 60 percent of their sales were overseas. They also had experience with foreign subsidiaries, for they had inherited a French company at the time of the original merger and then in 1924, after disposing of their French affiliate, they had opened a factory in China.

The decision to invest in Egyptian textile industrialization proved to be long, drawn out, and complex. In broad outlines it conforms to certain generalizations about direct foreign investment, but not so in many details. As for why Calico and the other firms were so late in creating overseas affiliates, the answer would appear to be that the firms were able to achieve rising rates of profitability, despite declining output, through the use of pricing combinations. It was under the pressure of the Depression that these arrangements broke down and that firms had to seek other means to generate profits. They were compelled to look to those areas in which most of their sales had traditionally occurred and where they had suffered severe market losses. But the finishing firms were at a disadvantage because they did not have their own merchants overseas; nor did they have trading and outlet subsidiaries as did many of the major British manufacturing concerns. Bradford, Calico, and Bleachers bleached, printed, and dyed on commission and were utterly dependent on cotton merchants (often called converters) to purchase cloth from the weaving companies and to sell the finished cloth in domestic or overseas markets.[25]

Calico, as the most diverse and vertically integrated of the printing firms, had its own merchandising department, however. Indeed, thirteen of the original companies were merchant firms, and they enabled Calico to market some of its cloth domestically. But overseas it relied on non-Calico men, especially in Egypt. Not surprisingly, the pressures to invest in Egypt did not originate with the Calico board. Its members lacked their own sources of information on what was happening there. The prodding came from their Egyptian merchandising agents. The triggers to invest were the conventional ones that often spur overseas investment decisions: the new Egyptian tariff barriers and the impending loss of a favored market. The selling agents sounded the alarm by spurning Calico products in favor of Japanese, Italian, and Indian goods. They ran up large debts to Calico, grumbled about the stodginess and uncompetitiveness of the Calico lines, and (among a small group of merchants deeply committed to Calico) suggested a Calico investment in Egypt's emerging textile industry.

Over the years Calico had created a large and complex network of local agents in Egypt. The home board was rightly troubled about losing their loyalty in the face of foreign and local competition. A report laid before the board in 1933 provides a glimpse of this once-efficient organization, now greatly in decline. The entire trade at this time was concentrated in the hands of a very few large-scale merchants based in Cairo. These merchants in turn had under them a group of smaller merchants, called travelers, who had responsibility for the distribution of the Calico products throughout the countryside (see table 2.5). The large merchants were extended substantial amounts of Calico credit. David Ades's account, for instance, was £60,000 in arrears in 1932. Ydlibi and Company owed £20,000, S. S. Sednaoui £7,000, and Btesh £38,000.[26]

Under foreign competition these merchants had begun to fall away, preferring the more popular products of non-British firms. Faced with the dilemma of losing its reliable distributors, Calico extended Btesh £25,000 additional credit despite his debt of £38,000 and a trading loss of £34,000 in the previous fiscal year. The Calico board was desperate to avoid being reduced to having David Ades as their only merchant in Egypt.[27] At the same time the board dispatched one of its own members, W. Buckley, to make an on-the-spot investigation of the financial and trading conditions there.[28]

Buckley went out to Egypt in 1933, with the hope of encouraging Calico's agents to take more of the Calico product and to publicize the virtues of British manufactures. He also intended to talk with government officials and leading businessmen about quotas for British textiles.[29] Yet from the moment he arrived, local industrialists and merchants besieged him with requests to establish a prints factory in Egypt.[30] The Calico board had already (in 1932) discussed such a project, rejecting a proposal from Arno Pearse, chief of the cotton sales department of the Misr Cotton Export Company and an adviser to the Committee of the Federation of Master Cotton Spinners and Manufacturers' Association, Manchester, to join with the Misr Spinning and Weaving Company in establishing a calico print works in the country.[31] The Misr leaders insisted on 51 percent control in any merger; Calico was unwilling to accept minority status. Buckley's conversations in Egypt, however, convinced him that Egypt was serious about textile industrialization. Foreign capital was certain to be drawn into the expansion of the industry.

Buckley's first report from Egypt painted a grim picture of Calico's trade competitiveness. The Japanese were underselling many of Calico's cotton lines by as much as 30 to 40 percent. In cut silks Japanese products were 60 percent cheaper than Calico's. Buckley warned that Calico could lose all its agents. Although he pursued trade quota discussions, seeking to persuade Egyptian government officials that Egypt should take a certain quantity of British textiles in order to assure the British market for raw Egyptian cotton, he was far from optimistic.[32] He was especially critical of Lancashire threats to boycott Egyptian cotton. While it was true that British firms were the major purchasers of Egyptian cotton (indeed approximately 15 percent of the raw cotton supply in the 1920s was Egyptian),[33] they were at the same time highly dependent on Egypt for high grade cotton for the high count, finely woven cloths. A boycott would injure British industry as much as the Egyptian cultivator and was likely to put Lancashire plants in the Bolton and Manchester districts out of business.

Other Calico board members and some of their Egyptian merchandising agents arrived at the same conclusion: to wit, trade quotas and threats of boycotts were mere palliatives. Calico could save its market in Egypt only by investing in Egyptian textile industrial development. A second Calico board member, N. G. McCulloch, writing from Egypt in May 1933, offered the first concrete proposal for a print works in Egypt.[34] By August the local merchant, Btesh, went further, recommending Calico's participation in a giant, vertically integrated textile conglomerate, which would involve the Misr Spinning and Weaving Company and Filature. The total capitalization was likely to be in the neighborhood of LE 1 million.[35]

At this early stage in Egypt's textile development the possibilities for expansion were numerous. Egypt's two modern firms produced a coarsely woven and inexpertly bleached cloth. The finishing of cotton piece goods through dyeing, bleaching, and printing had yet to occur. Nor did Egyptian firms produce high count and finely spun cloth. But although at first McCulloch's proposal for opening an independent print works may have been appealing, it took very little knowledge of the political and economic climate in Egypt to convince the Calico textile men that an independent company was likely to fail. Although the Lancashire firm possessed superior technical know-how, an independent British firm was unlikely to have influence with the Egyptian state. The third Calico board member to visit Egypt in 1933, Lennard Bolden, described the dilemma well: "Without political influence it would be difficult to start a works here as the authorities might prevent the staff landing or if landed remaining more than a short time."[36] He also anticipated that the company would have to pay "squeeze"

The question of investing in Egyptian textile development had some obvious drawbacks, and these were always prominent in the board's discussions. Participation in Egyptian industrialization would threaten Calico's merchant agents in the country and would arouse strong opposition from the entire Lancashire textile manufacturing community, eager to retain Egypt as an export area. Yet the board empowered its three members in Egypt—Buckley, McCulloch, and Bolden—to draw up detailed plans for a joint Egyptian venture. Spurning the more grandiose ideas for a huge textile conglomerate (one of which envisaged the merging of Calico and Bradford Dyers with a local firm backed by two leading Egyptian businessmen-politicians, Isma'il Sidqi and Ahmad 'Abbud), the Calico agents decided in favor of an alliance with Filature. Their conversations with merchants and the British Embassy staff, and their own investigations of Filature and Misr recommended Filature on the ground that the firm was "efficient and well managed in marked contrast with those controlled by native firms."[37] McCulloch's preference for Filature over Misr was undiluted. He regarded Filature as having "a good board of influential men who have struck me as sensible and reasonable and with whom we shall be able to get on."[38] Bolden had praise for Salvago and Barker, two of the Filature board members, and mentioned that the board also included O. J. Finney, reputed to be the wealthiest man in Egypt, and Elie N. Mosseri, whom he described as an Italian Jew, having all the permanent Egyptian government officials in his pay.[39] Mainly, however, the Calico people were attracted to Filature because of Linus Gasche, probably the most knowledgeable textile man in Egypt at the time.[40]

The single most important question to occupy the attention of Bolden, Buckley, and McCulloch was with what firm to align. Much less attention was devoted to other questions. Labor costs, market size, profitability of the enterprise, and prospects for expansion were all laid out in letters sent from Egypt to the board. But they did not receive detailed treatment. The board members in Egypt took it for granted that Egyptian textiles would have state support. Hence if Calico aligned with an efficient textile firm, the plant's long-run success would be assured. Moreover, their investigations were quite hurried. A spate of rumors had created a climate of business hysteria. The Calico representatives in Egypt were certain that the Italian firms Gnocchi and Meridionale were on the verge of consummating a deal in Egypt and would steal a march on them.[41] The Calico board moved hastily and without undertaking what today would be considered proper feasibility studies. Their financial plight at home made them desperate to find salvation abroad. They were given to flights of financial fancy about an Egyptian undertaking, the most recurrent and least grounded of which was a belief that the Egyptian textile industry would quickly dominate the local Egyptian market and then take over nearby Mediterranean and African markets.

These Calico men on the spot in Egypt who debated the question of investing in Egypt in no way resembled the hidebound and risk-averse businessmen portrayed in many studies of twentieth-century British businessmen.[42] If anything, they were too optimistic and casual about committing the home firm's resources to Egypt. Nor were they careful and rational profit maximizers, unprepared to venture capital without comprehensive planning. They were navigating quite uncharted economic and political waters in Egypt, compelled to rely on a few trusted advisers (the British commercial attaché, G. H. Selous, and their merchant-agents) and to make quick decisions before all the facts could be assembled. What finally disposed them to favor an Egyptian overture (and on these crucial issues they were largely right) was their certainty that Calico's Egyptian market was lost, that Gasche was a superior textile man, and that the Egyptian elite was committed to making textiles succeed.

At home, however, in the sober chambers of the Manchester board, the directors were less smitten by dreams of a vast Egyptian textile complex. What reconciled many of them—the merchanting and exporting divisions of the company—to an Egyptian investment was an understanding that the Calico plant in Egypt would print coarse and inexpertly woven Egyptian cloth which would not compete with the higher count grades and more finely spun cloths which Calico exported.

Nowhere in the Calico records (or later in the Bradford materials) is there any discussion of Britain's financial and political sway in Egypt. Yet British suzerainty weighed in the Calico and Bradford decisions to invest. To be sure, Egypt had been given nominal political independence in 1922. (The scope of this autonomy was extended by the Anglo-Egyptian Treaty of 1936.) But when conferring unilateral independence on Egypt in 1922, the British statesmen had reserved certain powers to themselves, of which defense, the protection of foreign interests, and imperial communications assuredly counted heavily for businessmen contemplating investment in that country.

Britain's economic and political sway in the 1930s could be seen in many concrete ways. Although the British army of occupation was limited to

10,000 men by the 1936 treaty and confined to the Suez Canal area (once suitable military accommodations had been created there), this number of troops was double that with which Lord Cromer had dominated Egypt in the heyday of Britain's imperial authority. Foreigners enjoyed inordinate protections and privileges as a result of the Capitulations, which were widely and generously interpreted in Egypt. These rulings ensured that the homes and business premises of foreigners were virtually inviolate. They could be entered or searched by the Egyptian government only after securing the consent of the foreign consul. Foreigners were tried either in their own consular courts (for criminal matters and personal or family law) or by the mixed tribunals (for civil offenses), where the majority of judges were foreign. No tax on a foreign person or establishment could be enacted by the Egyptian government without first securing the agreement of his government. In effect this particular aspect of the Capitulations limited the taxation of foreigners and foreign firms to a variety of relatively small items—the house tax and stamp duty. Not until just before the outbreak of World War II and after the Capitulations had been abolished (1937) was a tax on company profits introduced; only after the war did the state introduce a personal income tax.

Not only was Egypt an attractive investment area because of the lightness of tax and the political stability secured by an army of occupation, but as part of the sterling area Egyptian currency was freely exchangeable for British sterling. No currency controls existed in the 1930s although they were to be introduced during World War II. Egypt's most important bank, the National Bank of Egypt, a quasi-central bank and issuer of the local currency, was linked with the Bank of England. The National Bank of Egypt had two separate boards, one based in Egypt and headed in the 1930s by a British-trained banking official (Edward Cook) and a second, advisory board, sitting in London and working closely with the Bank of England and British government personnel. Although in all these respects Egypt was nominally independent, it was deeply enmeshed in Britain's imperial structures. Businessmen would have deemed it a safe investment area in the 1930s.

Indeed, Egypt had become an important British investment zone by the end of the nineteenth century, accounting for perhaps as much as 1.5 percent of all British overseas investment (approximately £43,753,000 out of a total of £3,191,836,000). This was a relatively high figure given the fact that Egypt was a small, underdeveloped country.[43] Until the 1930s British investment in Egypt was confined to a few well-demarcated areas, connected with the cultivation and export of cotton. British investors held a substantial portion of the Egyptian state debt, though less than the French. They were involved in banking through Barclays Bank, and in agriculture through land mortgage banking and land development companies. The British government itself held 44 percent of the shares of the Suez Canal Company. Through the Anglo-Egyptian Oil Company, a subsidiary of Shell Oil, Britain dominated oil exploration in the Eastern Desert and Sinai. But the only investment remotely related to industrialization was Britain's domination of Egypt's canal, barrage, and dam construction. Through the London Office of Consulting Engineers and through the placement of British advisers in the Egyptian Ministry of Public Works and the Egyptian Department of Irrigation, British construction firms monopolized the tenders put out for these lucrative undertakings. Although investment in Egyptian industrial development was a new departure for British businessmen, investors could take heart from the fact that the British and other European investors had already sunk vast amounts of capital in the country.

By the beginning of 1934 Bolden, who by then had taken the lead in the Calico negotiations, was thoroughly in favor of investing in Egyptian textile industrialization. In a long and detailed letter to the board in Manchester—a document which came close to representing a feasibility report—he laid out the financial and technical possibilities in Egypt. Spinning and weaving, he believed, would pay despite technical deficiencies in Egypt, so long as Egyptian duties were high. Printing would also pay, provided it was combined with spinning and weaving. The printing of imported cloths was unlikely to prove profitable, given the high level of duties and the limited Egyptian market. This advice ruled out a totally separate printing works (like those which Calico had in Lancashire) in favor of an integrated textile complex. No doubt this proposal had appeal to the Calico board since by the 1930s most British textile managers favored integrated complexes and attributed the decline of Lancashire to a surfeit of small, highly specialized firms. Finally, Bolden emphasized the virture of an alliance with Filature over the Misr Spinning and Weaving Company in large measure because of his confidence in Gasche. Bolden worried, however, that the chief subordinates at Filature under Gasche were hardly better than third-rate technicians and managers.[44]

The striking of a joint-venture bargain proved more difficult to consurnmate than either side anticipated. The negotiations took a full year. Many of the difficulties were predictable: amount of capitalization; management responsiblities; and length of the agreement. Yet the chief stumbling block proved to be the suspicion that each firm had of the other. Calico feared that Filature would enter the area of printing itself and become Calico's rival. Filature was concerned that the Calico alliance with Filature would be a mere stepping-stone to the establishment of a huge independent textile company in Egypt.

At first the Calico board considered the option of Calico's purchasing a proportion of the Filature shares. This was ruled out because the shares were overpriced. In any case Calico was opposed to accepting minority status with Filature.[45] Instead the two companies proposed to create an entirely new textile firm, jointly financed and managed by Calico and Filature. Mutual suspicions were removed by Calico promising not to compete with Filature in spinning and weaving, though it would be free to carry on its importing. Filature agreed not to start up a print factory for at least twenty years.

Signed in 1934, the agreement between Filature and Calico created a new Egyptian textile joint stock company, called Société Égyptienne des Industries Textiles (SEIT). The agreement was to run for twenty years. The new company would spin, weave, bleach, dye, and print. In short, in conjunction with Filature, which would do most of the spinning, it would be Egypt's first fully vertically integrated textile firm. The main office was to be in Alexandria. The plant was to be located at Karmuz, not far from the center of Alexandria and thus able to draw upon Egypt's large pool of skilled and unskilled textile workers in that growing industrial center. The capitalization of the company was fixed at LE 80,000, with each of the parent firms responsible for LE 40,000. The board of ten members was divided equally between Filature and Calico. The original capital outlay was used to purchase 500 looms, bleaching and dyeing machinery, and two printing machines. Gasche was named managing director of SEIT, and Filature was required to furnish the new plant with all the yarn needed to keep 500 looms working 12 hours a day and 6 days a week. Filature agreed to supply power and steam to SEIT which would sell its finished products through Filature's network of sales personnel. Any future expansion of the joint venture company would occur in proportions equally divided between the two parent firms.[46]

The details of the agreement are worth commenting on in light of certain criticisms made of multinationals operating in the Third World. Far from being permitted to establish a dominant position in the Egyptian textile sector, Calico entered Egypt in an almost diffident way, under the control of a local firm. While the capital and the board membership were equally divided, the crucial position in the new firm, that of managing director, was occupied by Linus Gasche, the managing director of Filature. Moreover, although Calico had five members on the board of SEIT, these men did not attend board meetings which took place in Egypt. The Calico board was unable to control the affairs of its Egyptian affiliate. Right from the outset Bolden identified the dilemma and hoped to be able to insinuate a Calico man into Gasche's presence.[47] But he did not succeed; SEIT remained very much under the control of Filature.

Nonetheless Bolden was profoundly optimistic about Egypt's textile prospects. The joint venture seemed to him a veritable coup, which through an incredibly small outlay, could stem the decline in Calico's position in Egypt and eventually lead to a lucrative export trade. In a letter to the home secretariat he characterized the new joint venture as "an experiment in printing at a cost to us of £40,000 which without their [Filature's] aid would cost us something like five times that amount as they are supplying all buildings, power, steam, and spinning, all except the last of which are supplied on terms better than I could have hoped for."[48]

Against the obvious advantages, however, had to be counted the opposition of many of Calico's selling agents in Egypt. They felt betrayed since Filature would market the SEIT production. The tendency for these local merchants to look elsewhere for their supplies was accelerated. Equally aggrieved were the Lancashire textile businessmen who were struggling to achieve unity in their ranks and hoped to negotiate special trade agreements with the Egyptian government.

The advantages that the creation of this new firm brought to Egyptian textile development were palpable. Far from taking Egyptian textile development off into unwanted directions or taking over a market which local industrialists could easily have exploited, Calico introduced finishing skills which the textile sector sorely needed. It also offered the prospect of producing finer quality, higher count cloth which the local industrialists had not yet manufactured.

Filature's position within the Egyptian textile community was greatly enhanced by the agreement. The new SEIT firm began its first printing operations in 1935.[49] Under prodding from Gasche and heightened tariffs, SEIT expanded its plant and its capitalization to LE 400,000 in 1935 and LE 500,000 at the end of 1938.[50] During the first capital expansion the Bleachers Association joined the venture by taking up LE 50,000 of the £320,000 increase in capital stock.[51] Bleachers provided expertise in the bleaching trade and thus enhanced the finishing capabilities of SEIT. As the capitalization expanded, so did the plant and its output. The number of looms rose from 500 to 2,000, and the bleaching, dyeing, and printing works were enlarged at a cost of LE 500,000. Even as Filature and SEIT emerged as the most heavily capitalized and productive textile complex in Egypt, the expansion caused severe problems in Lancashire. Gasche's insistence that SEIT serve as distributors of Calico products was accepted because of the partnership. Calico actually feared that Gasche would take over Calico's most successful designs and reproduce them in his plants in Egypt. Much more ominous was Gasche's pressure on the Egyptian government to heighten tariffs (raised significantly in 1935 and again in 1938) and his pressure on the Calico men to join in this campaign. Gasche, in fact, wanted precisely that which the home board had always feared: high tariffs on light, finely spun material, exactly those piece goods which Calico sold in the Egyptian market. Although the Calico members did not press the Egyptian government to raise tariffs, they invested more money in the Egyptian enterprise once the duties went up.

By 1938 Filature had stolen a march on its chief rival, the Misr Spinning and Weaving Company. Taken together, the two Filature firms in that year had a nominal equity capitalization of LE 987,500 and reserves totalling LE 236,529. The Misr Spinning and Weaving Company's nominal equity was LE 1 million, but its reserves at the end of that year had declined to LE 100,000.[52] Moreover Filature and SEIT had bleaching, dyeing, and printing capabilities, while Misr was only able to produce gray cotton piece goods. Filature also extended its vertical integration to the hosiery and apparel business. In 1934, Filature sank capital in the Société Égyptienne de Tissage et Tricotage and the Société Égyptienne d'Industrie de Tissus Éponges, two companies which specialized in weaving, doubling, bleaching, and dyeing. In the next year it helped to create a larger, more heavily capitalized knitwear company, merging a group of small apparel manufacturers (the proprietors of the Fabrique de Tricotage d'Égypte; Bauerle, Dorra, and Baur; Fabrique Chausettes; and Dorra Frères) to found the Société Égyptienne de l'Industrie de Bonneterie.[53] This firm with a capitalization of LE 50,000, half of which was subscribed by Filature, specialized in weaving, knitwear, hosiery, bleaching, and dyeing. Filature supplied much of the material.

Filature's growing position in the local market and its financial success in the late 1930s was attested to by rising dividends and increasing reserves. Although Filature did not make any dividend payments until 1931-32, it did so thereafter with regularity. Dividends rose from 5.85 percent in 1932-33 to 13.75 percent in 1938-39. They represented an 8.2 percent return on nominal capital and accumulated reserves between 1935-36 and 1939-40.[54]

Financial success was not achieved easily, however. Only in 1932-33 was the company able to pay off arrears to its preferential stockholders for the years 1927-28 to 1930-31. In the next fiscal year it finished paying preferential stock arrears.[55] In 1933 the company replaced most of its preferential stock bearing a 6.5 percent dividend with 25,000 ordinary shares, and subsequently it increased the capital of the company to LE 390,000.[56]

A Bradford Dyers director, H. R. Armitage, reported in 1936 that the Filature plant had 80,000 spindles of which one third were new and the rest in good working order. The bulk of the spinning frames had been supplied by

Platt Brothers. He added that the plant was generally in good working order and was better equipped than almost any mill in Lancashire.[57] Even more impressive to the Calico backers was the company's extensive sales network. While the firm sold about 5 percent of its production through its own fourteen shops, the remainder went to independent merchants in the larger towns who in turn sold to smaller merchants and shopkeepers. Filature's main agents included some of the individuals with whom Calico had once worked. The firms of Ades and Btesh qualified for as much as five months' credit from Filature; the average amount of credit was on a much smaller scale, however, fluctuating between £300 and £1,200.[58]

The Bradford-Misr Affiliation

The expansion of Filature and the joint venture with Calico displeased Tal'at Harb who was eager that the Misr complex be the leading textile enterprise in Egypt. The British commercial attaché, G. H. Selous, conveyed Harb's displeasure to the Manchester textile directors and advised a British alliance with the Misr empire.[59] Thus, considerable pressure continued to come from the Egyptian side, where the Misr executives were eager to align themselves with a foreign firm possessing sophisticated finishing skills.

By the time that Tal'at Harb struck his deal with Bradford Dyers, the Misr Spinning and Weaving Company had already become one of Egypt's largest and most heavily capitalized industrial firms. The Misr textile expansion had been rapid and difficult. Capitalization had risen from LE 300,000 in 1927 to LE 500,000 in 1933, LE 800,000 in 1934, and LE 1 million in 1936. The Misr Spinning and Weaving Company had also issued bonds worth LE 340,000 in 1934, LE 450,000 in 1935, and LE 200,000 in 1936, and had borrowed heavily from the parent Misr Bank.[60] The huge capitalization was employed primarily to purchase equipment from England. The company began with a modest 12,000 spindles and 484 looms, and produced its first cloth in December, 1930, just in time for the new tariff reform.[61] But anticipating a large expansion of textile production, the firm drew up plans for a group of separate but integrated factories for spinning, weaving, bleaching, dyeing, printing, and finishing. In 1933 the Misr Company made major purchases of secondhand equipment from three Lancashire cotton factories. A large Oldham firm of six mills supplied 96,000 spindles of the mule type and 50,000 spindles of the ring type. The Peterworth Hall Company of Milneborough supplied 97,000 mule spindles, and the John Whitaker Company at Stockport provided 35,000 spindles of the doubling type.[62] Negotiations continued for the purchase of additional spinning and weaving equipment from factories at Bolton and Farnworth.[63]

By the end of 1936 the Misr Spinning and Weaving Company had 44,000 spindles in its first spinning factory and another 82,000 in a second, with a third scheduled for completion by the end of 1937. In weaving, the firm had in place 862 looms and two separate plants by the end of 1936. Scheduled for completion by the end of 1937 was a third weaving factory with 2,300 looms.[64]

The expansion of the company's capital did not proceed smoothly, however. Whereas the company's first issue of capital (LE 300,000 in 1927) was oversubscribed, the effort to raise funds later, during the Depression, did not produce the same enthusiastic response. In 1931 a public subscription for the Misr Spinning and Weaving Company netted LE 154,140 out of the authorized £200,000.[65] In 1934 the public took up one third of the issue of LE 300,000, forcing Bank Misr to subscribe the rest.[66] Thus, the financial expansion of the Spinning and Weaving Company drew heavily on the resources of the parent firm. The Spinning and Weaving Company paid its first dividend in 1932 and continued to pay dividends each year thereafter. The bank in that year began to transfer its shares of the company from its investment account to its portfolio of disposable securities.[67] But its financial commitment to the Spinning and Weaving Company actually grew rather than declined. As late as 1959, just prior to its nationalization, Bank Misr held more than one million shares (or 26 percent) of the Misr Spinning and Weaving Company.[68]

Confidential reports filed in 1937 by A. L. Anderson and H. R. Armitage of Bradford Dyers showed the Spinning and Weaving Company to be a massive undertaking, full of weaknesses. The firm had 100,000 spindles and more than 6,500 employees. It was thought to have employed at some time virtually every male eight years of age and over in and around Mahalla. Despite Tal'at Harb's rosy prognostications, the site raised obstacles to development. Cotton had to be brought from Alexandria by canal and then hauled for nearly a mile over a very bad road. Fuel was brought in by road although special railway sidings were in the process of being erected. The labor supply was uncertain, hard to hold and to motivate. No doubt part of the problem stemmed from the exceedingly low wages: two to four piasters per day for boys of seven to eight years of age; three and a half piasters for unskilled adult males rising to six to seven piasters as workers became more proficient; and piece work rates for the most efficient workers. The company also employed about a hundred girls, mainly in doubling and hosiery. It used an elaborate and bitterly resented system of fines to control the labor force. A fine of three piasters, for example, was assessed for a small spinning or weaving error found in the examination room; five piasters for a medium error; and up to 20 percent of the value of the piece for a large error. There were also fines for negligence and disobedience. Some were as much as half a day's pay.[69]

The plant itself was far from modern; nor was the equipment in a good state of repair. Armitage of Bradford said that while Misr could make finely spun and côarsely spun cloth, the largest proportion of the finished cloth was coarse, not a pure white. Only one fifth of the spindles themselves were in good working order; two fifths were delapidated; and the remaining two fifths were fit only for scrap. He concluded that the bulk of the Misr plant was secondhand and should be replaced. "It was even worse than the average spinning plant in Lancashire."[70]

Without doubt the Misr Spinning and Weaving Company relied heavily on the state and other special supports at the outset. In addition to tariff duties, the company sold approximately one fifth of its total production to the government. The police and army purchased underclothes from the company, and the Agriculture Department used mesh cotton covers in fruit orchards.[71] Far more important to Misr and Filature was the state's agreement to sell stockpiled cotton to them at cheap rates. In return, these two firms were obligated to use the entire supply of government cotton over a three-year period, to employ three *qantars* of regular cotton for every seven *qantars* of government-supplied cotton, and to allow the state to share in the profits.[72] Lastly, the Misr and Filature firms negotiated a sales agreement which divided the market between them and restrained their competition. Their joint selling organization, called Comptoir de Ventes de Files, marketed all the yarn and almost all the cotton piece goods of the two firms. The only products sold separately were specialty items, which constituted at that time about 20 percent of their total production.[73]

Tal'at Harb's displeasure at being left behind and his growing willingness to strike bargains with foreign companies in the 1930s—after having eschewed these liaisons in the first decade of the bank's existence—opened up the possibility of a joint textile venture. The company which came forward was another British textile company hard hit by the depression: Bradford Dyers Association.

If Calico's financial condition in the 1930s was precarious, Bradford's was desperate. Having declined from being Britain's seventeenth most heavily capitalized manufacturing firm at the turn of the century to forty-seventh position in 1929, it found its export capacity and its ability to generate profits under heavy attack.[74] The company had a nominal capital of £4,808,031, consisting of £2,549,237 of five percent cumulative preference shares of £1 per share nominal value, and £2,258,031 ordinary shares of £1 per share. It incurred its first operating loss in 1930.[75] The board responded by cutting the ordinary dividend to five shillings per share and taking funds out of the reserve for the equalization of dividends. What was thought to be a temporary expedient became a regular practice. As further losses or miniscule profits were made, Bradford Dyers was forced to eliminate the dividend on its ordinary shares in 1932. It made no payment on its preference shares in that year. By 1938 the general reserve had been completely eliminated, and the accumulated claims of the preference stockholders were £765,000.[76] The *Investors Chronicle*, a respected financial journal, warned prospective investors that the purchase of Bradford Dyers Association stock—ordinary or preference shares—constituted "a highly speculative lock-up of funds" and pointed out that the ordinary stock had fallen from eleven shillings a share to four shillings and three pence and the preference shares from fifteen shillings to seven shillings in twelve months.[77]

Bradford's increasingly restive shareholders refused to accept chairman Douglas's explanation that Bradford's difficulties were owing to cutthroat competition at home and Japanese dumping abroad. They attributed the company's financial decline to board mismanagement. By the late 1930s they were in rebellion, although their only recourse was to raise protests at the annual stockholders' meetings since Douglas maintained firm control over the board and always had a majority of the stock to vote in his favor. The 1938 meeting was acrimonious. One of Douglas's critics charged the board with paying themselves high salaries and having too many old and unimaginative members. He ended his attack by complaining that "the balance sheet indicated gross mismanagement," and suggested that "the whole of the assets [of the company] were now the property of the debenture shareholders."[78]

Although Bradford did, in fact, have an overseas affiliate (its American firm was also losing money in the 1930s), it was at first less inclined than Calico to venture into the Third World. Despite the complaints of dissident shareholders it was more tightly run and specialized than Calico. Although its directors saw the virtues of integrated textile production, they themselves had little experience of it. More to the point, the firm had no liquid capital. Nonetheless, the directors were eager to consider proposals to stem the decline in exports. Egypt was a country whose market in black sateens Bradford had once completely dominated. Indeed, one whole factory in the Bradford complex, Cawley of Salford, produced nothing but black sateen cloth, mainly for purchase by the women of Egypt.[79]

Bradford Dyers entered Egypt in a more deliberate and planned way than Calico. The long-term results were to prove more satisfactory. While there were reports of a Bradford interest in Egypt in 1932 and 1933, the board did not make a serious overture until the end of 1935. The board discussed Egypt at a meeting in October, 1935. Its view of Egypt's development potential was less sanguine than that of Calico. The Bradford directors worried about the overall size of the Egyptian market. They feared that an investment in Egyptian industrialization would damage the British export effort to Egypt and would undercut those Egyptian merchant capitalists who had played such a prominent role in the Bradford trade in the past.[80] At a meeting in July 1936 the Bradford board ruled against an affiliation with Filature and Calico Printers "because of the unsound selling scheme . . . which was in opposition to the powerful Egyptian Jewish interests."[81]

In January 1936 James Butterworth, a board member and a specialist on the trade with Egypt, was sent out there.[82] His knowledge of the Egyptian trade had convinced him that Bradford exports to the country were doomed and had made him the most energetic apostle of investing in an Egyptian plant. The board instructed him to evaluate the textile conditions in Egypt, and if they looked promising, to acquire land suitable for the erection of a plant for spinning, weaving, and finishing. He returned after a first investigation and then went out again in November 1936, taking with him Anderson, an expert in the erection of textile plants.[83] In Egypt he sought the advice of Alexander Keown-Boyd, a former high-ranking British Embassy official and a man with an intimate knowledge of the Egyptian political scene. Although Keown-Boyd was neither a textile man nor a businessman, Butterworth believed that his contacts with the Egyptian government would prove invaluable.

At first Butterworth's idea was to create a vertically integrated textile complex, managed entirely by Bradford, and drawing upon local capital, particularly that of the local mercantile element. He envisaged a board, with Keown-Boyd as chairman and British directors to represent the spinning, weaving, dyeing, and finishing sections of the enterprise. The board would be rounded out by including "a Sidqi" and three or four other well-placed Egyptians, including a representative of the importers. No doubt Butterworth believed that the Egyptian representation would smooth the way with the government and would also encourage local investors to take shares in the company. Butterworth himself was willing to start the factory and to train a successor, but he refused to stay on in Egypt. He contemplated a large contingent of British managerial and technical personnel. He was, overall, sanguine about the development prospects, pointing out that there was no dyeing in Egypt, except of the "lowest grade yarn woven into the cheapest cloth and dyed at the cheapest rate."[84]

Butterworth's encomium did not persuade the board at home. Chairman Douglas saw this step as jeopardizing the Bradford export trade.

"It would be only a few years before the whole of our Egyptian trade would go."[85]

Questions were raised about the sources of capital. At home the leading advocate, H. R. Armitage, favored commencing with a dyehouse and moving gradually into spinning and weaving. When Douglas replied that the effort would cut Bradford's throat, Armitage countered that it was going to be cut anyway. Armitage was head of an aniline black dyeing plant in Bradford, which had specialized in the Egyptian trade and was badly hurt by the decline in overseas markets. He contemplated the transfer of his increasingly idled machinery to Egypt and the erection of an aniline black plant there.[86]

In February 1937 Anderson and Butterworth purchased land for a possible factory site from the Smouha estate not far from Alexandria. They had decided to locate at Alexandria only after a careful survey of other areas. Mahalla and Damanhur were ruled out because of the problem of labor supplies. Tanta was dirty and dusty and had inadequate access roads. Alexandria was preferred because of its proximity to labor and raw cotton and the chance to build up an export trade. Keown-Boyd identified Defichon on the Smouha estate as the ideal site for the factory. It had the advantage of being far enough removed from Alexandria to be away from its political pressures, but still close enough to attract labor. It was situated on the main road and had good road, rail, and water communications. It was only ten minutes by car from the municipal boundary. Cheap labor was readily available and skilled labor could be attracted from the Karmouz quarters of Alexandria. Smouha was prepared to sell a slice of his estate in return for shares in the new company.[87]

The only problem with the site was obtaining government permission for the discharge of the factory's crude effluent into Lake Maryut. Fishing on the lake provided a livelihood for a nearby community and food for the inhabitants of Alexandria. Here the Bradford delegates were brought face to face with the government. "One thing apparent," Anderson wrote to the board, "is that to ensure success from the start we must have the support of the permanent officials in the government as these are the persons who count." The first meeting with the undersecretary of state for public works, Husayn Sirri, did not go well. Anderson described him as "exceedingly curt". He granted permission to take water from the Mahmudiyah canal but not to discharge effluent into Lake Maryut. Subsequently, however, Keown-Boyd put Anderson and Butterworth in touch with Hasan Rif'at, undersecretary of state for the Ministry of the Interior. Rif'at was more encouraging and promised the Bradford men a solution to the Lake Maryut problem.[88]

In keeping with their deliberate approach to investing in Egypt, Bradford commissioned a detailed feasibility study. The investigation was carried out by one of their local merchants, quite possibly Leon Belilos, who had a detailed knowledge of local manufacturing conditions. His conclusion was that given Egypt's large demand for textiles and the completely inadequate industrial plant in existence at the time, an important opportunity for new investment existed. The labor costs were cheap by international standards, even for skilled workers, and the government would provide customs protection. In short, an integrated cotton textile project was "favored by the local production of the best cotton in the world, by the newest and most modern industrial plant, etc., by fifteen million resident consumers of uniform qualities. . . ."[89] Even the board at home was impressed, and while they were not certain how lucrative the Egyptian market might be, they were optimistic that an efficient textile complex could build up an export trade to the countries situated at the eastern end of the Mediterranean. The board contemplated spending £700,000, even £1 million. One member expatiated that Egypt's export trade in the Mediterranean might well in time amount to five or six times the volume of the Egyptian home trade.[90]

There were notes of caution. The board concluded that while Egyptian textile exports would entail savings in transportation costs to the eastern Mediterranean, many of the other costs, like electricity and even some forms of skilled labor, were not cheap in Egypt. Questions were raised about how Egypt would entice neighboring countries to buy Egyptian textiles when Egypt bought nothing from them.

The Bradford scheme for investment was based largely on plans for the transfer to Egypt of plants idled by the decline of Britain's export trade. Bradford intended to erect the sateen manufacturing plant of Wainman Company Limited of Nelson and the Cawley dyeing machinery there. Even at this late stage in the investment scheme, when British agents had begun to secure permits to erect their factories, Bradford contemplated an entirely independent operation. What finally persuaded the board to form an alliance with the Misr Spinning and Weaving Company was advice from men on the spot, financial difficulties at home, and a more realistic view of the Egyptian political climate.

From the moment the Bradford contingent arrived in Egypt the British commercial attaché, Selous, had counseled an affiliation with Misr. He was under no illusion about the efficiency of the Misr companies, which he, like other foreigners, scorned. But he recognized the preeminent position that the Misr family of firms had achieved in the political economy, and the harm that Misr and its political allies could do to any British investment which they opposed. This advice was echoed by Edward Cook, governor of the National Bank of Egypt and even by Keown-Boyd, who was working closely with Misr personages like Sadiq Wahba and Ahmad 'Abd al-Wahhab. Keown-Boyd summed up this point of view well when he wrote: "The Bank Misr has now become so much of a popular institution and is so generally known as a patriotic affair that anyone who can be said to be running against it in any way is bound to incur the extremes of unpopularity, even though he may have government support." Keown-Boyd advised Bradford Dyers to invite Tal'at Harb to Manchester and concluded that while Tal'at Harb "has only the dimmest and most elementary ideas on the whole subject [of textile development] · · · he is determined that· nothing should be done unless he has a finger in it."[91]

A second and closely related factor was the difficulty in raising the necessary capital for an independent venture. Most of the capital would be raised locally since the Bradford firm itself lacked start-up capital. Yet without Bank Misr participation the local board was unlikely to have impressive directors and might well fail to generate the necessary capital. Finally the local political situation gave pause. The board's conclusion concerning the primacy of politics drove inexorably toward an alliance with Misr: "We think it should be kept in view if the scheme goes forward that we are establishing ourselves in a country where the sanctions which regulate the conduct of governments and ministries are much less firmly established than they are with us."[92]

The negotiations, opened in 1937, proved "prolonged and tiresome".[93] They did not produce an agreement until late in 1938. At home the moving force continued to be H. R. Armitage who envisaged a technically sophisticated plant. Eschewing the Calico preference for manufacturing coarse and simple lines, not likely to be competitive with Lancashire imports, Armitage saw that textile development in Egypt would lead inevitably to full self-sufficiency and the elimination of all textile imports, save for luxury items. Although he believed that the plant would start by finishing imported gray piece goods, he expected Egypt to be producing its own gray piece goods within a short time. For Egypt to be a lucrative investment area, the new plant there must manufacture imported styles, even those from Lancashire, including mercerized and schreinered sateens, schreinered colored twills, heavy merinos, nainsocks, lawns, and voiles.[94] Armitage's insistence on puttng the Bradford plant at Egypt's technical frontier was a shrewd one. The Bradford affiliate erected the most modern and the most profitable textile plant in Egypt.

In March 1938 Tal'at Harb and the Bradford Dyers' directors consummated their agreement. It was more elaborate and carefully drawn than the Calico-Filature treaty. Once again both sides were suspicious of the other's ambitions and sought to write safeguards into the charter. Bradford and Bank Misr agreed to create two separate textile companies. The first, called the Misr Fine Spinning and Weaving Company, was located at Kafr al-Dawar. It had a capitalization of LE 250,000 of which LE 200,000 came from Bank Misr and its affiliates and LE 50,000 from Bradford Dyers. It also had a mixed Bradford-Misr board of directors. The Misr Fine Spinning and Weaving Company was to spin and weave fine gray cloths from Egyptian cotton suitable for the class of goods to be dyed and finished by the Bradford Dyers affiliate. This company, called Beida Dyers, was also located at Kafr al-Dawar. It too had a capitalization of LE 250,000, of which Bradford contributed £200,000 and Bank Misr LE 50,000. Like the Misr Fine Spinning and Weaving Company its directorate was a mixed Bradford and Misr one, with the Bradford element assumed to be in the majority. Beida Dyers was to bleach, dye, and finish Egyptian cotton goods of fine weaving. It was to have the capacity to handle 6,000 ninety-yard pieces per week—the exact output which the Misr Fine Spinning and Weaving plant was responsible for producing. The charter was to last for thirty years.[95]

Just before the final signing of the agreements Tal'at Harb with two of his top officials (Ahmad 'Abd al-Wahhab, a financial expert, and 'Abd al-Rahman Hamada, head of the Misr Spinning and Weaving Company at al-Mahalla al-Kubra) met with the Bradford directors in Manchester. Subsequently, Armitage, Keown-Boyd, and Butterworth met with Smouha, Ades, and Rofe in London and extracted promises from these individuals of personal and financial support. The commitment of Ades and Rofe was significant, not only because of their financial contribution but also because they represented a powerful Egyptian mercantile element whose allegiance Bradford wanted to maintain.[96]

The new Beida factory was less grandiose than earlier Bradford schemes had envisaged. It had the advantage, however, of not obligating Bradford to provide the one commodity which was in short supply—cash. Very little liquid capital went into the Beida company. The hundred-feddan estate purchased from Smouha was paid for by Beida shares; an overwhelmingly high proportion of the LE 250,000 capitalization took the form of Bradford machinery, dismantled in England and reassembled in Egypt. Much of the machinery, like the Cawley plant, was already idled or scheduled to be put out of operation.

In 1939 the first British contingent of managers and technical experts arrived in Egypt. There were less than a dozen, although by the standards of Egyptian joint-stock ventures this group constituted a large foreign presence. G. W. Bird, one of the group, provides a good estimate of their abilities. At the management level Alexander Keown-Boyd was designated chairman with Charles Butterworth as deputy chairman. Neither man knew the technical aspects of finishing—a responsibility which devolved on the eight British technicians, including Bird. Bird, an expert in finishing cloth, had gained his apprenticeship at Salford (Cawleys) in a plant specializing in dyeing blacks, mainly for the Egyptian market. He was joined in Egypt by Charles Thresh who was in charge of dyeing and bleaching. Each had an assistant. A production manager, a chief engineer, a foreman fitter, and a making-up department foreman constituted the rest of the British technical staff. Most of the machinery installed in the factory was quite old-fashioned, but in Bird's opinion satisfactory, and an advance on anything that Egypt possessed at the time.[97]

Was the bargain a good one for Egypt and its future textile development? Two opposite and competing views were enunciated at the time. They continue to echo in debates over foreign investment. The Alexandria Chamber of Commerce, an Egyptian business group (and perhaps somewhat hostile to the Misr organization), railed against Bradford's entry. They argued that while Bradford specialized in work not being done in Egypt, in fact the existence of the Beida factory made it difficult for Egyptian businessmen to establish purely Egyptian plants in these the more specialized branches of textile production.[98] Tal'at Harb, in his speech to the shareholders of Bank Misr following the agreement, called the arrangement an unabashed triumph for emerging Egyptian capitalism. He pointed out that the bank had blocked Bradford's independent entry into Egypt and at the same time had brought into the country a firm with impressive technical, productive, and managerial skills.[99]

The final assessment of this arrangement and of its benefits and drawbacks has to be made on the basis of the firm's operation over the entire course of its existence (see chapter 3). At the outset, at least, the bank had stymied a Bradford effort to create a wholly independent, vertically integrated textile complex of considerable size (perhaps £1 million) and influence. Also, Beida, like SEIT, provided Egypt with finishing skills not available in the country and enabled the Misr complex to establish a fine spinning plant.

The Partnerships Begin

Critics of direct foreign investment contend that outside investment skews the direction of economic development, encouraging the manufacture of products not essential to the masses, albeit attractive to the upper classes because of status appeal, and implants an inappropriate, capital-intensive mode of factory production. But such complaints against Bradford and Calico are not entirely valid. The obvious next stage in Egyptian textile development was fine spinning, fine weaving, and the finishing processes (bleaching, dyeing, and printing). Both Calico and Bradford brought these skills. Their contribution took the form of technicians and plant. Most of the liquid capital, however, was raised in Egypt while the capital equipment came from England.

On the question of the appropriateness of the imported technology, it may be said that the "indigenous" Egyptian textile factories had already established heavily capitalized firms by 1930. They were growing in the 1930s. These firms were large because a few well-connected businessmen stole a march on the field, creating firms before the tariff reform of 1930. One of these men, Tal'at Harb, was enamored of size and had an unmatched capacity to mobilize substantial amounts of capital. The British firms, then, entered a business environment of largeness and concentration. Far from displeasing them, these factors were sources of gratification. British directors espoused integration and concentration and attributed the decline of the domestic industry to excessive competition, the smallness of units, and the lack of integration. They valued Egypt because it offered them an opportunity to create the kind of textile industry which they had been unable to establish in Britain. To be precise, they were attracted by the prospect of having easy access to the government. They preferred an industry dominated by a few integrated and financially powerful firms, able to set output targets and prices and thus not subject to the unregulated competition and overproduction which many of the British textile magnates believed was the source of the decline of the British industry. No doubt they also believed that a nonunionized Egyptian labor force would keep labor costs low although so far as we can tell, the British firms had made no detailed investigations of the cost of skilled and unskilled labor in Egypt.

While the British operatives hoped to create integrated management structures, they imported into Egypt a textile technology, even the very machines, used at home. Although the equipment was not the most advanced, it was more sophisticated than anything Egypt had at the time. But the British managers were not inflexible in using Egyptian labor on these machines. They strove for high capital intensity, but they were mindful that Egyptian labor was cheaper and less skilled. They accepted the higher labor to machine ratios existing in Egypt. Egyptian industry in 1939 required fifteen to eighteen workers per thousand spindles, compared with 4.2 in Europe and the United States. The textile managers in Egypt pointed with pride to the fact that these ratios had been eighteen to twenty-four workers per thousand spindless less than a decade earlier.[100]

Tal'at Harb had had a vision of creating a wholly Egyptian-owned and Egyptian-managed textile industry. These joint venture enterprises (SEIT and Beida) marked the end of this dream. No doubt had the pace of textile industrialization been a slower one and had the two British firms not moved so aggressively, albeit under prodding from local businessmen, to enter the Egyptian industrial sector, the Misr textile complex might have continued to be a predominantly national one. Tal'at Harb might well have bought the technology at arm's length and retained total managerial control as he did when he established the Misr Spinning and Weaving Company. But the pressure from the British firms could hardly be resisted in a semicolonial territory ruled by the British themselves. Thus it was the British—their managers and technicians as well as their machinery—who arrived in Egypt and created the new joint ventures. The intention of the parent firms was to have a coterie of directors, managers, and technical experts in Egypt at all times. This proved exceedingly difficult to achieve, but at all moments there were always a few British textile men in Egypt, overseeing aspects of the investment there.

In the negotiations over the terms of entry into Egypt the government did not play a major role as governments often do in settings where special concessions for mines, public utilities, and banks are concerned. For Calico and Bradford the Egyptian government hovered in the background, always a threat to their plans. The actual negotiations were carried out with Egyptian business leaders. The British directors were aware of the government's presence, nonetheless. They had to secure visas for employees, residence permits, and various kinds of licenses. They were conscious that they were entering a strange and in many ways potentially hostile political economy where economic nationalist sentiments could be aroused. Their protection was to be their alliances with well-established local firms. Linus Gasche and Tal'at Harb rather than the Egyptian minister of finance and the Egyptian minister of industry decided the terms of corporate entry into Egypt. These shrewd Egyptian-domiciled businessmen drove effective bargains.

The evolving textile industry in Egypt did, however, have drawbacks, characteristic of the Egyptian firms as well as their foreign affiliates. The expansion of modern firms was at the expense of artisans. It was also at the expense of the poorer classes who would have been able to purchase cheap Japanese, Italian, and Indian textiles except for the high tariff barriers.

Another obvious and immediate disadvantage was that foreign firms set the tempo of textile expansion in Egypt. Fine spinning, weaving, and expert finishing were the obvious next stage of development. British investment ensured that foreign capital would play a leading role in this evolution. At a slower and more controlled pace Egyptians would have moved into these finishing industries as they did after World War II. In addition, in order to retain an involvement in textile expansion the two local firms had to stretch their financial resources to dangerous levels. Filature managed to increase its capital despite a difficult transition in the early 1930s. Bank Misr's eagerness to remain the unquestioned giant in the textile field forced it to take financial risks. The bank's overextension was exposed by a depositors' run in September 1939, at the onset of World War II.

Recent interpretations of the Bank Misr crisis of 1939 attribute the bank's difficulties to mismanagement of funds, corruption, and the extravagant provision of loans to politicians and wealthy landowners.[101] An equally important factor was an increased commitment to textile development, a commitment which culminated in 1938 and 1939 in the creation of the Misr Fine Spinning and Weaving Company, a partial interest in Beida Dyers, and the provision of a LE 2 million loan to the Misr Spinning and Weaving Company.[102] Although the bank's investments proved lucrative ones in the long run, they locked up huge amounts of the capital of the bank and its depositors' resources.

The Egyptian textile industry made remarkable strides in the 1930s but was also beset by problems. In 1930–31 Egyptian manufacturers, artisanal and modern, consumed only 1 percent of the entire domestic cotton crop (78,000 *qantars* out of 8,276,000 *qantars*); by 1940–41 the proportion had risen to 9 percent (826,000 *qantars* out of 9,169,000 *qantars*).[103] The local production of cotton textiles also rose from 12 percent of local consumption in 1931 to 75 percent in 1941. The most rapid advances occurred in 1938 and 1939, following immediately on the large tariff increase in 1938. During these two years Egypt's production of cotton piece goods rose by 66 and 45 percent respectively; the quantity of imported cotton piece goods declined by 19 percent and 40 percent. Until 1938 the import of cotton piece goods had remained fairly stable, fluctuating during the 1930s between a high of 193,403,415 square meters in 1935 and a low of 147,004,859 square meters in 1931. Thereafter it fell precipitously. (See table 2.6.)

The three integrated textile complexes established their dominance in yarn production and cotton piece goods in the 1930s. In 1940–41 Filature, with its affiliate Société Égyptienne des Industries Textiles; the Misr Spinning and Weaving Company; and the Misr Fine Spinning and Weaving Company, with its affiliate Beida Dyers used 700,000 *qantars* of the 826,000 *qantars* consumed domestically. They produced 26,000 tons of cotton yarn out of a total of 32,500 (roughly 80 percent). Their weaving output of 100 million square meters was 50 percent of the total.[104] Obviously some leeway existed for smaller, less heavily capitalized, and more specialized weaving firms. Spinning, however, was the domain of the giants. Of these big firms the Misr Spinning and Weaving Company had reclaimed its preeminence and was responsible for over half of Egyptian yarn and one third of locally-produced cotton piece goods.[105]

By the outbreak of World War II Egypt ranked twenty-second in the world by number of spindles (354,000 in 1943–44, of which Filature and the Misr Spinning and Weaving Company each had over 100,000), and twentieth by number of looms. The achievement must not be exaggerated, however, since Egypt's yarn production constituted a mere 0.56 percent of world production, its spindles only 0.22 percent of the world's total, and its weaving machines only 0.25 percent. While Egypt consumed about 826,000 *qantars* of cotton in its local factories, Indian spinners spun fifteen to twenty million *qantars* per year, and Americans thirty-four million.[106]

Despite the rapid growth of the textile industry and the growing profitability of its firms, the industry had yet to deal with its most serious problem: the factories' obligation to use locally grown cotton. In most countries it would be an advantage to have local cotton; but the kinds of cotton cultivated in Egypt were precisely the wrong kinds for the country's textile development. Egyptian cotton was of high quality and long staple, in demand in Britain and continental Europe, where it was spun at high counts and made into fine cloth. But these luxury cotton pieces were of little interest to the ordinary Egyptian consumer who wanted the cheaper cloths, spun coarsely and at lower counts. Moreover, the new factories in Egypt, utilizing a simple technology, specialized in coarse, low counts. Yet Law No. 1 of 1916 made it illegal to import raw cotton. Designed to keep cotton pests and diseases out of the country, the law barred Egyptian textile manufacturers from using cheap American and Indian cottons which would have been far more suitable for the cloth they wanted to sell in Egypt. In the 1930s threads from count number four to count number fifty constituted more than 90 percent of total Egyptian production. Indian cotton was well suited up to number sixteen and American cotton ideal from sixteen to thirty. Local factories, however, were compelled to use Ashmuni cotton, the cheapest and least high quality of the Egyptian cottons. The result was that Egyptian thread cost 10 to 40 percent more than that manufactured from Indian or American cotton.[107] To reserve the local market for local production the state had to erect high tariff barriers against cheap textile imports and sacrifice the poorer consumers who were unable to afford the expensive Egyptian-made piece goods.

The alternative of developing a higher-grade textile industry for sale to Egyptian wealthy classes and ultimately for export had little appeal at this stage. The Egyptian middle class was small; the Egyptian manufacturers had yet to master the technology of this production. Indeed, the only firm which produced threads above count number fifty was the Misr Fine Spinning and Weaving Company.

3

Textile Development
1940-1956

In their entry and their first half-decade of business activity in Egypt (1935–40) the British textile firms did not establish a privileged position for themselves or deflect the pathway of Egyptian textile development already forged by local business elites. The next decade and a half (1940–56) saw no alteration in these power relationships and patterns. If anything, the influence of the Egyptian partners (Misr and Filature) grew at the expense of the metropolitan firms and their Egyptian affiliates (Beida and SEIT). Increasingly the fundamental textile decisions in Egypt were made by the local businessmen with scant regard for the wishes of the boards in Britain.

In the post-war decade Egypt proved to be a less lucrative investment area than originally anticipated, especially as expectations of ultimately breaking into export markets vanished. As a result the British firms sought to curtail their involvement there, even to extract themselves altogether, but they did not succeed. Rising nationalist sentiment and fears of nationalization and expropriation spurred efforts to reduce their exposure in Egypt. Yet altering the original financial arrangements proved exceedingly difficult. By the mid-1950s, just prior to Egyptianization in 1956, the Lancashire records suggest that the periphery had succeeded in gaining an upper hand over the metropole. Local business executives dominated the joint ventures and employed British capital for their own purposes.

In order to place the experience of the two British joint ventures (Beida and SEIT) in perspective we need to look at the general evolution of Egyptian textiles during the boom years of World War II and the textile slowdown, even crisis, after the war. A survey of Egyptian textile development will enable us to judge the effectiveness of the Beida and SEIT plants as well as to compare the one foreign affiliate with the other.

Wartime Textile Development

Dependency theorists argue that Western political and economic crises—world wars and global depressions—offer brief but important opportunities for structural economic change in the periphery of the world economy. World War II enabled the Egyptian textile industry to increase its capitalization, its profitability, its output, and its employment numbers. By the end of the war the textile industry had consolidated its place as one of the predominant industries in Egypt, the others being foodstuffs preparation and construction. Yet from a longer-term perspective (even into the 1950s) the war-induced textile development produced deep-seated problems. It crvstallized an uncompetitive but powerful industry. Textile industrialists came to look to the state for support, and the state in its turn expected much from them. The tension leading up to the military revolt of 1952 and the expropriation first of foreign business concerns and then Egyptian businesses owed much to the artificial and uncontrolled industrial expansion during World War II.

The most obvious indication of industrial growth for Egyptian textiles lay in increased output. The war brought a sharp reduction in textile imports and at the same time a large increase in local demand, fuelled by the allied troops stationed in Egypt. In 1938 Egypt imported LE 3,339,000 of cotton textiles, constituting 9 percent of the value of all Egyptian imports. By 1943 this figure had fallen to LE 1,848,000 (5 percent of total value), and though the value in current prices rose to LE 4,837,000 in 1949, this figure constituted only 3 percent of the value of all Egyptian imports.[1] According to a United Nations report, Egyptian imports of cotton fabrics fell from 13,270 metric tons in 1938–39 to 3,880 metric tons in 1948–50 and 860 metric tons in 1954–56.[2] Domestic output increased as local industrialists sought to overcome the shortfall in imports. Starting from a production of 93 million square meters in 1938 local firms increased their output of woven cotton fabrics at a rate of 10 percent per year during the war. By 1946 domestic production stood at 195 million square meters per year; only 10 percent of textiles sold in Egypt came from foreign sources.[3] The country had become nearly self-sufficient in the production of cotton yarn (see table 3.1).

The five major cotton spinning and weaving firms on which we have been focusing (Beida, SEIT, Filature, the Misr Spinning and Weaving Company, and the Misr Fine Spinning and Weaving Company) played a decisive role in this expansion. The total production of cotton yarn by the Misr Spinning and Weaving Company and the Misr Fine Spinning and Weaving Company rose from 16,349,661 kilograms in 1940 to 23,818,015 in 1945–46, and their production of cotton piece goods increased from 93,388,050 yards in 1940 to 135,362,634 yards in 1945–46. These outputs constituted approximately 45 percent increases in yard and cotton piece goods production (see table 3.2). SEIT's weaving production went from 23,757,236 yards in 1939–40 to 30,046,083 in 1945–46, of which nearly half the output was printed. The value of its sales increased fivefold, from LE 736,447 in 1939–40 to LE 3,443,571 in 1945–46, while its use of thread expanded by more than 60 percent between 1943–44 and 1945–46.[4]

Expanded output came from increased use of existing plant rather than plant expansion or modernization. Under wartime pressure, plants ran continuously for twenty-four hours a day and six or seven days a week. The British-administered Middle East Supply Center, based in Cairo and overseeing the economic planning for the entire Middle East, blocked the creation of new plants and the importation of new machinery. The supply center was committed to the efficient use of existing resources and to the reservation of shipping space for essential exports and imports. By the middle of the war the Misr Spinning and Weaving Company at Mahalla was burning *mazout* (the residue of refined petroleum) because of shortages of coal and oil, and by war's end most equipment was worn out from extended use, and desperately needed to be replaced.[5]

Although the large established firms maintained their share of the local market, the increased local demand and the unavailability of imports opened up opportunities for other companies and individual artisans. In 1939 there were only eight other textile firms besides the five already discussed. Their combined capitalization was a mere LE 393,000. Most of these under-capitalized firms were in the clothing and apparel end of the trade and did not compete directly with the major firms in yarn production and cotton piece output. By 1946, however, five new textile firms had appeared, and the total capitalization of these five plus the eight which had been in existence before 1939 had grown to LE 3,207,000. Several of the companies had a full complement of spindles and power looms and were prepared to compete with Misr and Filature as integrated cotton manufacturing complexes. In particular the Nile Textile Company and the Société Industrielle des Fils et Textiles hoped to use wartime circumstances and postwar reconstruction to enter the textile sector as major firms. (See table 3.3.)

By 1947 textiles employed 100,312 workmen compared with 36,276 in 1937.[6] This sector was the leading industrial employer, offering work to 48 percent of the total industrial work force employed in medium- and large-scale establishments (those with more than ten employees).[7] The amount of capital employed in textile production in 1947, according to the Census of Industrial and Commercial Production of that year, was LE 25,102,620 or 21.4 percent of all industrial capital.[8] This figure gave textiles second ranking to food processing, but it represented a large increase over the previous census when textiles had registered LE 3,602,375 capitalization: 11.5 percent of the total in industrial establishments.[9]

Rising production translated itself into heightened profits and dividends. For the major textile firms the war years were little short of a financial bonanza. The capitalization of the five big companies grew by a modest 10 percent but the reserves of four of them (those for which we have detailed information) went from LE 326,082 in 1939 to LE 5,428,215 by the end of the war. Net profits, which had been 7.6 percent of nominal capital and reserves (LE 242,870) increased to LE 1,264,972, or 15.6 percent of capital and reserves. Dividends rose from 8.4 percent of nominal capital in 1939 to 35.6 percent of capital in 1945. Part of the huge increase, however, was owing to firms being unable to replace worn-out equipment or keep their stock of spare parts at high levels. (See tables 3.4, 3.5, and 3.6.)

The new competitor firms also enjoyed financial success. For the eight firms for which we have reasonable statistical data the return on capital and accumulated reserves at the end of the war was slightly better than that of the giants: 18.5 percent as compared with 15.6 percent (see tables 3.7 and 3.8).

These impressive statistics concealed severe problems, however, created in large measure by the forced pace of industrial expansion. In an almost totally protected market companies sold everything they produced, with the allied armies taking commodities priced beyond the purchasing capabilities of Egyptians. Wooden spindles and antiquated looms were pressed into service. Artisans thrown out of work in the 1930s resumed their trade. Numerous poorly managed firms came into existence.[10] By the end of the war these companies had swelled the ranks of textile producers and were influential in political discourse. They defended textile interests vigorously, drawing powerful support from the Egyptian Federation of Industries. Moreover, the state now considered a large labor-employing textile sector essential to Egypt's economic and social well-being. It turned a blind eye to the fact that the industry consisted of a motley array of small artisans and over-capitalized and poorly administered firms. Various minority and Wafdist governments, holding power between 1945 and 1952, feared the revolutionary consequences of any large reduction of the work force and sought to prop this sector up rather than forcing it to rationalize.

Another set of problems which emerged from the war was to plague the textile industry in the post-war period. They stemmed from the governmental effort to regulate the prices and output of the textile factories. The Middle East Supply Center, in assuming far-reaching powers over the Egyptian economy, introduced a comprehensive set of controls over the textile sector in November 1940.[11] Price regulations proved to be a constant source of complaint and in time became the bane of the industrialists. Ostensibly the state sought to maximize local production and ensure widespread distribution of cloth. In fact pricing never worked effectively or gained wide support. At first regulated prices provoked bitter protest from the merchant community of Alexandria. Through the Alexandria Chamber of Commerce merchants complained that the prices fixed by the state were higher than those in the open market. The controls merely served as a pretext for the weaving firms to raise their prices. Subsequently and throughout the war the industrialists argued that the state commandeered too much of their production for popular cloth (as much as 75 percent) and did not allow the regulated prices to rise in keeping with increasing costs of production.[12]

The petitions against price control became insistent by the end of the war. The Misr Spinning and Weaving Company claimed that the policy was misguided and forced textile production into the wrong lines of production. By not allowing an increase in the price of people's cloth since September 1942, the state obligated textile operatives to sell nearly three quarters of their production at a loss or at a very small profit, and encouraged the development of a black market.[13] The company also complained that industrialists had to market the remaining quarter of production—mainly the more finely spun cloth destined for the wealthier classes—at inflated prices in order to cover deficits in popular cloth production. This arrangement made it difficult for firms to perfect their skills in high quality production, for which many believed that Egyptian industry had a comparative advantage because of the availability of locally-grown long-staple cotton.

In light of the profits being made by the textile firms and the explosive growth of reserves, these protestations hardly seem credible. In any case, the wartime controls were not removed at the end of the war. Textile leaders intensified their criticism of the state, claiming that these regulations forced the industry into directions for which it was not well suited and held back the development of the higher grade lines.

During the war the state also set levels of textile production, its goal being to maximize output and secure national self-sufficiency. The government's first target of five square meters of cloth per person per year in the urban areas and two and a half square meters in the countryside was derisory, and was revised upwards to seven square meters per person. Even so, as the economists of the British Middle East Supply Center conceded, seven square meters did not constitute a minimum standard, and they recognized that in the poorer rural areas large numbers would not have enough to clothe themselves and their family members. To make even this inadequate supply available, the state had to requisition 75 percent (and in certain years even more) of the total cotton piece goods production.[14]

Postwar Textile Expansion and Difficulties

The drawbacks and defects of the cotton industry notwithstanding, textile industrialists were filled with optimism as the war drew to a close. The general, industry-wide statistics suggested that the textile sector had overcome its weakness. Yet a closer examination, especially focusing on the level of the individual firm, reveals that the defects persisted. Let us, first, catalogue the signs of progress, as revealed in rising production, increased capitalization, and creation of new companies. Production figures were at high levels. In 1946, for example, the Misr Spinning and Weaving Company achieved record production figures: 19,000,000 kilograms of thread and 94,000,000 yards of weaving from 500,000 *qantars* of raw cotton. Tal'at Harb's dream of making Mahalla the Manchester of Egypt seemed well on its way to realization. The factories there employed over 25,000 workers and had 165,264 ring spindles and 3,992 power looms.[15] Firms had an abundance of cash. They contemplated using their cash reserves to modernize and expand. Merchants and large landowners were now eager to channel assets into this sector which seemed to offer returns as promising as agriculture and commerce. A seemingly vast export arena existed in the eastern Mediterranean and parts of Africa.

In the first few years following the close of the war numerous new textile plans were elaborated, and new plants came into existence. The major firms led the way, determined as they were to maintain market predominance. The Misr group, eager to draw upon Egyptian sterling resources accumulated in Britain during the war, announced a plan for importing the most modern spinning and weaving equipment. The Misr plant at Mahalla expected to spend LE 250,000 each year for five years on new equipment.[16] The Misr group was keen to maintain its reputation for producing the finest quality yarn in the Middle East and the highest quality and most finely spun cotton piece goods. The Misr complex at Kafr al-Dawar, including Beida Dyers, signed a contract in 1945 with British firms for the supply of 60,000 spindles and 1,280 of the most up-to-date British Northrup looms.[17] In 1943 the Misr Fine Spinning and Weaving plant had 44,500 spindles and 1,206 automatic looms. With its postwar expansion it forecast a plant of 100,000 spindles and 2,500 looms.[18] Meantime, Beida, in an effort to keep pace with its affiliate, built a completely new second plant. It had twice the floor area of the original plant, and new machinery; it was designed to handle the anticipated increase in output from the Misr factories. [19] Filature and SEIT also expanded, albeit not at such a rapid pace. They were content to allow the Misr firms to control a larger share of the local market. Between 1947 and 1950 SEIT built a new dyehouse, engraving block, and laboratory, and expanded its finishing and printing plant.[20]

The plans for plant modernization and expansion were based on the belief that Egyptian textile production could be dynamic and profitable, that the industry could dominate the local market where businessmen expected a flurry of buying following the close of the war, and that the visions of Mediterranean and African export markets were within reach. In the five years following the ending of the war the five major firms increased their capitalization by LE 2 million (or 60 percent). Their total nominal capitalization grew to LE 5,280,000. They also reduced their reserves by LE 700,000 as part of their effort at plant modernization and expansion. The reserves had, of course, increased disproportionately during the war, not merely because of large profits, but also because equipment replacement, except of the most vital kind, could not occur. (See table 3.9.)

Expansion was not limited to these five firms. In the two years immediately following the close of the war, fifteen new limited textile companies came into being (with a capitalization of LE 3.75 million), while sixteen already established companies increased their capital by just under LE 2 million. In 1946 alone the value of imports of machines and looms for weaving was over LE 1 million.[21] A group of new, aspiring textile giants emerged, prepared to compete with the Misr-Filature complex for market predominance. The major new firms founded in the postwar period were: the Fayoum Textile Company, created in 1946 with a capital of LE 400,000; Selected Textile Industries, which took over a small textile firm in 1946 and increased its capitalization from LE 300,000 to LE 500,000; al-Tawil Spinning and Weaving Company (1946) with a start-up capital of LE 250,000, increased to LE 500,000 in 1949; Société Égyptienne "Nouzha" de Filature et de Tissage (1946), with a capitalization of LE 300,000, increased to LE 400,000 in 1951; and Société des Usines el-Shourbagui pour la Filature, le Tissage, et le Tricot (1948), with a capitalization of LE 500,000. These firms had a smaller capitalization than Misr and Filature, and they did not have the large financial reserves to call upon which the older firms possessed. But their boards boasted important merchants (Ahmad al-Farghali), leading politicians (Muhammad Husayn Haykal), and numerous wealthy landowners, alive now to the possibilities of diversifying their assets.

Other firms which had already come into existence during or even before World War II also increased their financial assets, the most notable being Établissements Industriels pour la Soie et le Coton (LE 30,000 in 1942 to LE 400,000 in 1945 and LE 600,000 in 1948), the Nile Textile Company (LE 20,000 in 1941 to LE 200,000 in 1945 and LE 400,000 in 1946), and Société Industrielle des Fils et Textiles, Spahi (LE 20,000 in 1944 to LE 250,000 in 1945 and LE 1 million in 1947).[22]

All these firms were joint stock companies, the shares of which traded on the stock exchange. The information available about them is substantial since they were obliged by law to file annual financial reports with the Egyptian Ministry of Industry and Commerce and with their shareholders. Other forms of company organization, popular as late as the 1930s—private companies, partnerships, and unincorporated closely held family firms—had nearly all been transformed into joint stock companies because of the decisive advantages these companies enjoyed in wide access to capital and limited liability status. Thus, the figures available on the joint stock companies cover most of the modern textile production of Egypt.

The grandiose thinking of the immediate postwar period was exemplified by the Établissements Industriels Pour la Soie et le Coton. This company, which had had a mere LE 15,000 of capital in 1942, aspired now to join the Misr giants. Its founder and joint managing director, François Tagher, was trained in many branches of textiles in Lancashire, having lived in Bolton during the 1930s. He persuaded his wealthy father to back him in establishing a spinning and weaving company. Although he started very small, the war years were a boon. The capitalization grew to LE 400,000 in 1945, and LE 112,618 was accumulated in reserves. Already at this stage the Tagher firm owned a cotton spinning factory at Shubra Bahtum, a flax spinning factory at Shubra Bahtum, a mechanical weaving factory at Shubra al-Kheima, mechanical weaving factories at Shubra Village, and hand weaving plants at Daher.

Tagher succeeded more handsomely than the other newcomers. He could claim in 1955 that he had become the third most important textile manufacturer, ranking behind Mahalla and Kafr al-Dawar and in front of Filature. He boasted of having 15 percent of Egypt's total spinning capacity and insisted that the secret of his success was keeping the plant up to date and appointing as directors only fully trained technicians.[23]

The most spectacular breakthrough in textiles occurred in rayon production. The major textile firms in Egypt (Filature, Misr, and Beida) and many important Egyptian businessmen and investors signed an agreement with the international engineering firm run by the von Kohorn family to establish the Misr Rayon Company. The von Kohorns were experts in rayon production processes and had assembled plants all over the world. Oscar, a 1903 graduate of the Textile Technological Institute in Chemnitz, Germany, originally developed processes for the spinning of carpets from cow, goat, and calf hair. Next he worked on synthetic fabrics and patented rayon-producing machines. The possessor of innumerable patents, the von Kohorns had opened plants in western and eastern Europe, Japan, and Latin America before their involvement in Egypt.[24]

The prospect of a large rayon complex, located near the Misr Fine Spinning and Weaving Company and Beida Dyers at Kafr al-Dawar and having a large production intended eventually for export throughout the Middle East, excited Egyptian investors. The von Kohorns' access to American technology and capital lent creditworthiness to the project. Knowledgeable Egyptian investors realized that the von Kohorn firm would be able to import American textile machinery, which was difficult to procure because of currency constraints. The LE 750,000 shares made available to the Egyptian investing public were oversubscribed by twenty-two times (at LE 17,163,644).[25] The popular response showed Egypt's abundance of capital, provided that a project caught the eye of the investor. But Egyptian investors were not energetic in searching for obscure investment opportunities, preferring to back well-known firms, well-established industries, like textiles, and highly publicized endeavors.

The Misr Rayon Company was created in 1946, with a subscribed capital of LE 1 million. The machinery, supplied from the United States through the von Kohorn group, was expected to produce five tons of thread and one ton of cellophane a day.[26] As an immediate goal the firm sought to satisfy Egypt's domestic requirements; its long-range goal was to export to neighboring markets.

The new firm did not progress rapidly. Machinery was slow in arriving, and the costs were greater than anticipated. The board opted to increase the capitalization by LE 1 million and issued LE 500,000 in stock and LE 1 million in bonds. The first production commenced in 1948.[27] The company made rapid progress thereafter, manufacturing rayon and nylon filaments, viscose staple fiber, nylon staple fiber, and transparent fiber. By 1956 the Misr Rayon Company had become the third most heavily capitalized textile company in the country (having a total nominal capital and accumulated reserves of LE 3,822,493), behind only the Misr Spinning and Weaving Company (LE 10,242,295) and the Misr Fine Spinning and Weaving Company (LE 8,367,115), but ahead of other large firms like Beida Dyers (LE 3,814,168), SEIT, and Selected Textile Industries Association (LE 1,102,107).[28]

The tricotage and apparel industries kept pace with general textile development. Although most of the clothes-making in Egypt was carried out in small-scale workshops of nine employees or less, a thriving incorporated sector also existed, specializing in the manufacture of undergarments, stockings, socks, ribbons, and lace. In 1948 the Ministry of Commerce and Industry estimated that tricotage factories and workshops employed 6,000 workmen and produced 70 percent of local consumption.[29] The renewal of imports following the war hurt these firms, however. Their products were not price-competitive, largely because the inputs of raw and spun cotton were expensive. Like the other textile operatives they pressured the government to make cheap cotton available. They also called upon the state to enact a ban against the import of underclothes, socks, and cotton stockings. The protest, representing the larger and more heavily capitalized firms, was channeled through the Egyptian Federation of Industries. The large companies also called on the state to regulate the smaller workshops, which they claimed used sweated and unregulated labor in order to undersell the larger, more carefully regulated competitors.[30]

All this postwar activity enabled textiles to retain their centrality in Egypt's industrialization effort. The production of the modern textile factories outpaced other industries in the decade after the war. Their output increased at a rate of 7.8 percent between 1946 and 1956, compared with 5.4 percent for the manufacturing sector in general.[31] In the 1950s the modern textile factories employed 150,000 persons, roughly 43 percent of all wage labor in medium- and large-scale establishments.[32] The textile factories had 612,000 spindles, more than three quarters of which were British, and 16,000 mechanical and automatic looms, and used 20 percent of the cotton grown in Egypt.[33] The country was becoming self-sufficient in textiles, from the most coarsely spun cloth which most firms had produced during the 1930s, to the higher grade, more finely spun fabrics which had for so long been the preserve of more advanced countries like Britain. The total equity capitalization and reserves of the twenty-eight textile firms catalogued in the *Stock Exchange Yearbook of Egypt* was LE 40,324,618 in 1956, and marked a significant rise over the nominal capitalization and reserves of the eighteen firms listed at the end of World War II (LE 15,257,224).

Yet these favorable industry-wide statistics, compiled by the state and industry representatives and carefully analyzed in numerous authoritative economic studies, do not provide the whole story. The balance sheets and annual reports of individual firms, the reports in the financial press of Egypt, and the unpublished business record of the firms themselves demonstrate that the industry was far from well-off. While there were wide variations within the general sector and between individual firms, the textile sector had not become the leading force for industrial development and economic progress. Companies tended to be greatly overcapitalized, with the most profitable firms accumulating vast and largely idle financial reserves. By the mid-1950s nearly all the firms were afflicted by declining profit rates, excess capacity, and overproduction. As the confidential British reports made clear, the industry had not expanded its domestic market as briskly as it had thought possible, and it had failed to break into foreign markets.

A brief look at the development of Egypt's postwar textile industry—drawing mainly on disaggregated firm statistics and records rather than the less revealing industry-wide composite data—will highlight the major difficulties facing this sector and will give a framework for evaluating the activities of the two British affiliates in Egypt.

The annual stockholders' reports of the firms reveal a clear dividing line between the five textile giants (the two Misr spinning and weaving companies, Beida Dyers, Filature, and SEIT) and the rest of the field. In addition to their greater capitalization, they continued to dominate production and to be powerful politically. Still, although the major firms enjoyed greater financial success than their new competitors, their returns on capital could only be deemed adequate. These were inferior to the projections made by industry optimists, and their decline in the 1950s was a source of worry. Four of the five firms for which we have data realized a higher rate of return on nominal capital and accumulated reserves in 1951 than they had achieved at the end of the war (13.5 percent vs. 12.6 percent), but the return fell to 9.2 percent by 1956. The companies' vast accumulation of financial reserves (LE 18,903,578) was three times what it had been in 1951, just after the large plant expansion and modernization had occurred. But the reserves signaled a blockage of development, rather than economic success, in light of the constrained domestic sales, overproduction, and failure to enter foreign markets. (See tables 3.9, 3.10.)

Less heavily capitalized concerns had significantly worse financial records than the giants. By and large the most successful businesses were those which endeavored to fit into safe niches of the textile sector and not compete with the giants. The firm which posted the most consistent profit record was Fabrique Égyptienne des Textiles, "Ka-Bo", specialists in cotton spinning, knitting, dyeing, and hosiery manufacture. Almost as successful was the Société Égyptienne de Filature et Tissage de Laine, which specialised in wool production, a field of much less importance to the majors. The only other firm to post high profit margins, al-Tawil Spinning and Weaving Company, was an integrated cotton textile plant, with substantially less capital than Misr and Filature, and content to manufacture some of the higher count, more finely spun cotton lines for which there was considerable Egyptian demand. The Tawil factory of 8,000 spindles was able to produce yarn ranging from twelve counts to eighty. As for the other lesser firms, few escaped fiscal years in which they recorded losses (in contrast with the majors where only SEIT posted a loss, in 1952). Indeed, the only firms to avoid losses were the Usines Textiles al-Kahira, which was a small company (128 looms) specializing in silk weaving; the Alexandria Spinning and

Weaving Company; al-Tawil Spinning and Weaving Company; Fabrique Égyptienne de Filature et Tissage de Laine; the Misr Rayon Company; and the United Spinning and Weaving Company. But none of the lesser firms had profit rates of the same order as the majors. None accumulated reserves like the Misr textile companies. Indeed in the troubled year of 1951–52 no fewer than ten of the twenty-two firms listed in the *Stock Exchange Yearbook* lost money. (See tables 3.11 and 3.12.)

Even some of the production data were disappointing. The most reliable statistics were those issued by the two major integrated cotton textile industries: the Misr Spinning and Weaving Company at al-Mahalla al-Kubra and the Misr Fine Spinning and Weaving Company. They were believed to produce 45 percent of all yarn manufactured and two thirds of all woven cotton fabrics. The Misr Spinning and Weaving Company was the larger of the two by a wide margin, spinning two and a half times as much yarn as its affiliate and manufacturing more yardage of cotton piece goods (two and a half times more in 1946 and 50 percent more in 1956).

The Misr Spinning and Weaving firms's output was clearly below projections. It rose approximately 33 percent over the period 1946 to 1956. On the other hand, its affiliate, the Misr Fine Spinning and Weaving Company, which, of course, specialized in high count, finely spun cloth, experienced the kind of explosive growth which the textile operatives had forecast for the entire industry. The firm tripled its yarn production and quadrupled its output of woven cotton between 1946 and 1956. (See table 3.2.)

The reasons for the textile slowdown, evident in the early 1950s, were multifaceted and affected nearly every area of the industry: productivity, management, trade and fiscal policy, labor relations, and industry relations with the state. In the first place the industry suffered grievously from excessive production, stemming in part from the large number of factories and their large capacity in relation to the purchasing power of Egyptian consumers. Textile enterprises had simply expanded too rapidly during the war and the immediate postwar years. Although production doubled during the war, in response to demand, production levels were maintained and even increased after the war. Sales did not keep pace. In 1947, for instance, the local consumption was 45,000 tons but production was 51,000 tons.[34] In the next year although consumption rose to 51,000 tons production increased to 55,000 tons.[35]

Trade and fiscal policies, particularly associated with British sterling, inhibited the industry's efforts to modernize after the war. The ambitious plans for using large sterling balances to purchase modern equipment could not be realized because of British currency controls. At first the British released sterling only at a trickle. Even after the Egyptians had left the sterling zone (in 1947), Britain's suspension of convertability restricted Egypt's ability to acquire dollars and make purchases from the United States. Egyptian firms complained constantly of British manufacturers' inability to deliver the machinery contracted for. By 1948–49 the problem of reequipment had become acute, and the Egyptian firms, in their protests to the British Embassy, claimed that the future of the industry was in jeopardy. In December 1948 for instance, the director of the Misr Spinning and Weaving Company complained that his firm had received only 520 looms of the 4,000 which it had been promised would arrive in a steady flow between 1946 and 1949. The Misr Fine Spinning and Weaving Company, better supplied, expected to have all its contracted looms by the end of 1949, the target date for delivery.[36]

The Misr firm directed its protest in the first instance at the British Northrop Loom Company, its primary supplier. Under heavy pressure from British firms at home, Northrop was only able to allocate an output of 500 to 600 looms from its annual production to the two Misr firms.[37] Unfortunately at this rate the Misr companies would be unable to reequip themselves before the fifties. The possibility of purchasing machinery in the United States, where the war had not destroyed industrial facilities, was ruled out because Egypt did not have a favorable trade balance with the United States and was prevented by British monetary restrictions from transferring sterling into dollars.

In many of the British textile business records the role of the Egyptian state looms large. Its influence was a mixed one for the textile sector, far from the strongly supportive position which the British businessmen had assumed would be taken when they first contemplated investing in Egypt in the 1930s. Indeed, the negative policies (price controls, pressures to increase production and employment, and insistence on using Egyptian cotton rather than cheap imported raw cotton) outweighed the benefits (tariff protection, encouragement of combination, and taxation policy), at least in the minds of the leaders in the industry. This situation should not have surprised the industrialists, since the state had always had a stronger commitment to other groups, especially the landlord lobby, and was growing apprehensive of the radicalism of disaffected workers and students.

The state, with its desire that the textile sector maintain a large labor force, made overproduction inevitable. Through legislation, though mainly by persuasion, it restrained the textile firms from dismantling the large textile labor levies assembled during and just after the war. The business firms and the financial press lodged a steady stream of complaints about surplus labor and inability to discharge workers. The labor law of 1944 on the hiring and firing of workers was not a stringent one, though it was amended and made tougher in 1952. It allowed firms to hire workers for a probationary period of six months, sometimes even a year, and it imposed relatively small severance indemnities on firms for the discharge, with justification, of permanent workers. The Misr firms seem to have avoided the problems of excessive work force in any case. The Misr Spinning and Weaving Company doubled its production and decreased its labor force by 40 percent in the decade after the war, and the Misr Fine Spinning and Weaving Company tripled production without adding to its labor force.[38] Perhaps the non-Misr companies—Beida, Filature, and SEIT—came under heavier government pressure to maintain their labor forces.

Poor labor-management relations afflicted the textile sector and added to problems of productivity and price competitiveness. All the major plants suffered debilitating strikes: Filature in 1946; Mahalla during September 1947. The reasons for the strikes were not confined to wage issues, though wages were central to all the disputes. Real wages had declined sharply during the war and only began to rise in the mid-1950s.[39] In Shubra, socialist and communist leaders stirred up and organized the textile workers, who rose to protest efforts to discharge leftist workers or those involved in union activities.

Labor-management tension at Mahalla was of a different nature. Here the work force was more removed from leftist ideological centers, although labor organizers did create an independent trade union there. Problems stemmed from the autocratic nature of the management and glaring income inequalities between workers and managers. In an effort to discipline untutored peasants, the Mahalla plant had introduced an elaborate system of fines for workers' infractions. These were a source of great and growing resentment. So too were the appalling living conditions at Mahalla where workers were crammed twenty to a room, in stark contrast to the homes of the leading executives, whose splendor rivalled those of European and North American businessmen. These homes cost upwards of LE 7,000, an extravagant sum for an Egyptian dwelling at the time. Managers also had access to elaborate sporting and recreational facilities and commanded substantial bonuses, the largest being LE 12,000 paid to the managing director, 'Abd al-Rahman Hamada.[40] Thus it was not difficult for union devotees to create a genuine workers' union.

Tariffication continued into the postwar period, in spite of the government's wartime promise to end controls. The state retained the system because it feared social discontent and wanted the rank and file to have access to cheap cloth. No doubt had the state truly wanted to ensure cheap cotton pieces it would have allowed the free import of Japanese, Italian, and Indian products. But the government's commitment to an indigenous textile industry stood in the way. The resulting tension came to a head whenever the textile leaders thought their profit margins were threatened. In 1945 and 1946, for example, businessmen complained that they lost money on popular lines.[41] The state responded by lifting the price of popular cloth but only by one piaster per meter, which the industrialists regarded as inadequate.[42]

The criticisms of tariffication were threefold. First, the industrialists complained that price controls existed on an excessive amount of their final product (still as much as 75 percent). The textile men asked for a reduction to 50 percent or less. But the postwar governments—Wafdist and minority ministries alike—refused, believing that the living conditions in Egypt, already below any minimally accepted level for many people, were driving inexorably toward revolution. A second complaint was that the high proportion of regulated production kept firms from developing the high quality, finely spun lines for which Egyptian industries might well have a competitive advantage. A third concern was the inability of the state (due to lack of funds and staff) to regulate smaller establishments, which as a consequence were free to produce the lucrative higher grade textiles.[43] Just how valid this last complaint was is difficult to determine. Probably the output of small workshops did not constitute a real threat to the big firms.

The state's role in textile production was a forceful and large one. Although the operatives assailed the state for its pricing and labor policies, the industry also depended on its favor. Heavy dependence on state assistance was an obvious and glaring flaw in the industry. Rather than becoming more efficient and more competitive with the passage of time, as was expected of nascent industries, textiles became increasingly reliant on the state, especially for tariff protection. Egyptian customs duties were raised yet again in the late 1940s and early 1950s to heights not anticipated at the industry's onset.[44] The politicians had struck a bargain with the industrialists whereby the textile companies produced substantial supplies of popular cloth and hired large numbers of workers, while the state gave the local market over to their manufactures, guaranteeing a profit margin on popular cloth and offering no objection to large profits on high quality products and the accumulation of vast financial reserves. But the bargain enabled jerry-built wartime firms to stay in existence, and kept the more efficiently run companies from feeling healthy pressures of competition.

Other forms of state help were equally important, yet often exceedingly deleterious. Mindful that the industrialists were prevented from importing cheap cotton, the state sold its own often substantial cotton stocks to the big firms at subsidized prices.[45] When it lacked such supplies, it provided subsidies to the weaving companies, paid out of the export tax on raw cotton.[46] In 1953 the state created the Caisse de Consolidation de l'Industrie de la Filature et du Tissage du Coton and used the funds of this organization to sponsor research and to provide export subsidies for surplus production. Parliamentary leaders justified these expenditures on the grounds that the textile industry was at a disadvantage in having to use expensive local Egyptian cotton. All these otherwise useful and beneficial programs increased the power of the government and induced businessmen to look to the state for their financial well-being.

Even though textile leaders railed against the state for its pricing policies and blamed the government for keeping the industry from expanding its production, even a cursory look at the balance sheets of the Filature and Misr companies reveals that these firms, including their British affiliates, were far from dynamic. These industrialists restrained the expansion of their own industry. They preferred safe and guaranteed profits and did not attempt to win new consumers at home among the poorer classes. Nor did they break into foreign markets. The large firms accumulated huge reserves in the postwar years and paid out a high proportion of their profits in dividend payments. Between 1946 and 1956 the four firms on average paid out 75 percent of their profits in dividends, with Beida Dyers and the Misr Spinning and Weaving Company leading the way with payments averaging 86 and 82 percent of net profits respectively (see table 3.13). Had these companies been willing to reduce the pay-out rate as well as the growth of their reserves (which were only infrequently employed for new projects), they could have sold popular cloth at lower prices and tapped a much larger domestic market. They could also have attempted to be more price-competitive in foreign markets.

A core difficulty was the continued obligation of textile manufacturers to use only Egyptian cotton to produce the coarsely spun cotton piece goods destined for the Egyptian masses. Just how much the use of Egyptian cotton added to the costs of production was by this time a hotly debated issue. According to the *Économiste égyptien*, an influential mercantile publication, raw material costs were a small fraction of the overall costs of production. According to the same journal, the cost of transporting raw cotton from India balanced the gain from using Indian cotton.[47] Most expert opinion differed from this view. In its report for 1948–49 the Misr Spinning and Weaving Company argued that the cost of cotton constituted no less than 60 percent of the retail price.[48] Writing during the war, an Egyptian textile expert, André Eman, estimated that Egyptian thread cost 10 to 40 percent more than that manufactured from Indian or American cotton and added substantially to the price the Egyptian consumer had to pay for cotton pieces.[49]

In truth the textile industry had been established on the wrong footing and needed fundamental change. Ashil Siqali, a member of the board of the Egyptian Sisal Company, offered a number of incisive comments on the problems besetting the industry. Opposing the suggestion that Egyptian textile firms needed high tariff barriers and export subsidies, Siqali pointed out that most of the present difficulties had arisen because of the artificial and breakneck textile expansion of World War II. New firms created during the war lacked good equipment, good managers, and skilled workmen. Siqali recommended a severe weeding out via market pressures. Inefficient producers would be driven into bankruptcy, leaving only those capable of producing in a cost-conscious way. To combat social discontent he favored the import of cheap textiles and the transformation of the domestic industry to the manufacture of fine cotton mainly for export. In this area Egypt had a natural advantage since its cultivators grew the highest quality long-staple cotton in the world.[50]

Ibrahim Salih, another Egyptian textile expert, echoed these sentiments. He argued that Egypt needed radical new departures in its textile production in order to overcome the mistakes made earlier. His most emphatic recommendation was that one third of the factories be permitted to import cotton to make cheap piece goods. The other factories should be encouraged to develop the fine spinning and weaving industry.[51]

The British Firms at Home and in Egypt

Within a palpably troubled business environment the two British concerns had widely different experiences in the decade following World War II. Beida Dyers took control of the high quality cotton piece goods market, expanded its production, and achieved high rates of return (high enough to enhance the financial well-being of the parent firm). The Société Égyptienne des Industries Textiles suffered grievously from overproduction, rising costs of production, and declining profit margins. Both parent firms worried about Egypt's political stability and the future of private enterprise in the country. They endeavored to reduce their financial exposure and to find purchasers for all or part of their assets. Bradford Dyers succeeded in selling off a large portion of its Beida shares to the Misr Spinning and Weaving Company (and almost managed to repatriate its money, but was stymied by an Egyptianization order following the British-French-Israeli invasion of the country in 1956). Calico was unable to find a buyer for its assets and came to regard SEIT as a bad investment over which the parent board had little control.

Both the war and the overseas investments helped to restore Calico to a reasonably good financial position. By 1945–46 Calico had paid off arrears on its preference stock, and in 1947–48 it rewarded its long-suffering and occasionally impatient ordinary shareholders with a dividend of 5 percent (on nominal value of the stock). It followed this pay-out with dividend payments of 8 percent in 1948–49 and 12.5 percent in 1949–50.[52] Even while these dividends were declared, the Calico board replenished its reserve funds, badly depleted during the depression years. The capital reserve had stood at £1.1 million in 1939 and the general reserve account was £450,000. Both accounts grew at rapid rates and by 1951 the Calico reserves totaled almost £10 million.[53]

The Calico decision to invest in Egypt in the 1930s was the second overseas investment choice, following the erection of a factory in China in the 1920s. The early efforts inspired others, so that by the close of World War II the company had wholly or partly owned affiliates in India, Australia, South Africa, and Indonesia as well as Egypt and China. So pleased was the board with the diversification that its members were ready to explore other opportunities.

According to the 1945–46 report, about £2.5 million of the company's £14 million assets were located in these overseas affiliates.[54] In 1947 the chairman of the Calico board, Lennox Lee, carried out a major overhaul of the board structure to reflect Calico's greater overseas presence and its evolution toward a multinational presence. Lee had long believed that the Calico board suffered from unclear and divided leadership and was asked to deal with detailed and technical matters for which it lacked expertise. In the 1947 restructuring, Lee confined the board's jurisdiction to broad policy issues. The ordinary administration of Calico was turned over to more specialized management committees. Lee's new board of directors was composed of a chairman (himself), a deputy chairman, and the managing directors of the five executive groups: works, commission printing, merchanting, mills, and overseas. The board concerned itself with high-level policy decision and left to the management committees the responsibility for the implementation of general policy and day-to-day administration. Increasingly, as more of Calico's resources went overseas, the overseas management committee assumed a dominant role in board discussions.

The reorganized board no longer had a single goal, as it had had before 1914 (printing on commission). It was now concerned with highly diverse and even incompatible interests. While the parent firm was eager to sell Manchester prints all over the world, it was also interested in establishing integrated textile factories abroad. The overseas management branch put pressure on the board to open factories abroad. On the other hand the commission printing and merchanting committees still wanted to preserve the rest of the world for Manchester exports. Lee's reform was intended to allow the full board to rule on these complicated and conflicting policy questions. But he was aware that Calico was being driven inexorably into the rest of the world, and he admitted at the time of the reform that the overseas management group had already established itself as the dominant faction in the corporation.

Although Egypt was one of the first overseas enterprises for Calico and one for which the board had high hopes in the 1930s, the opinion of the board had changed dramatically by the end of World War II. By 1945 Calico had come to the conclusion that SEIT needed major transformations to make it profitable and that Egypt was no longer an attractive investment area. The parent firm discussed its financial exposure.

The problems facing Calico in Egypt were legion. They began at the management level where Calico complained that the Bleachers Association, holder of 12.5 percent of the affiliated Egyptian company (SEIT), was nothing more than a "sleeping partner", content to receive dividend payments yet unwilling to be involved in the operation of the company.[55]

Calico's chief management complaint, however, was directed against Linus Gasche, who had been the primary reason for Calico's aligning with Filature originally. While conceding that Gasche was still the most knowledgeable textile man in Egypt, the Calico board grew resentful of his autocratic ways. Gasche failed to consult with his Manchester partner and simply announced important policy changes. Calico was annoyed that the decision to designate Robert Gasche, the son, as Gasche's eventual successor was made in 1950 without consultation. So distant was the Calico board from Egyptian affairs that only one of the British directors of SEIT received copies of the SEIT minutes.[56]

In the 1930s the Calico board members had vaguely anticipated this difficulty. They had hoped to introduce their own staff into the SEIT company. They even planned to send out a young textile man in hopes that he would learn the Egyptian business in great detail and become Gasche's chief subordinate and eventual successor. The ambition was not realized. The home firm was able to find only a few people for posting to Egypt, most of whom refused to stay more than a year or two. No British technician or manager ever succeeded in holding a high managerial position in SEIT or in taking any power away from Linus Gasche. In fact, when N. G. McCulloch went to Egypt in 1950, his visit was the first made by a Calico board member since McCulloch himself had been in the country in 1935 to negotiate the original agreement.[57]

No doubt the Calico board would not have expressed growing discontent about their Egyptian company had the balance sheets remained strong. But SEIT was afflicted with the same general problems which beset Egypt's textile industry as a whole. The labor situation was a particularly troubling problem. Labor-management relations had deteriorated badly after the war and had a substantial impact on output. A serious strike took place in July 1946.[58] In 1948 an alarming 41 percent fall-off in the production of the weaving shed occurred, partly because of the shortening of the working day from eleven to eight hours, but also because of repeated labor differences, marked by workers regularly downing their tools each day for half an hour.[59] In the opinion of the Calico board, government regulations exacerbated both labor tensions and labor inefficiency. The state required all firms to hire a high proportion of Egyptians not only in the regular work force but also in technical and managerial positions. The Company Law of 1947, which most foreign-owned businesses opposed, stipulated that companies operating in Egypt would have to offer 40 percent of their directorships to Egyptians, make available 50 percent of their shareholdings to Egyptian investors, and reserve 90 percent of work places to Egyptian nationals. The Calico board saw these restrictions as driving overseas capital away from Egypt and inhibiting firms from employing the foreign managers and technicians they needed.

The nationalist movement in Egypt, of which the Company Law was but one obvious manifestation, troubled the Manchester firm. Its effects were felt at many levels. Administratively, the parent firm complained about Egyptian governmental restrictions on European salaries and the red tape in obtaining residence permits.[60] But the company worried more about larger policy matters, the most ominous of which was the prospect that radical nationalists would come to power in a political and social revolution and dispossess private foreign firms. Although the Calico board did not have an intelligence department and thus did not know the details of the rising power of extreme right-wing and left-wing elements in Egypt, they did know that Egypt's political future was an unsure one and that the severity of social and economic problems made a cataclysmic political revolution a distinct possibility. Long before the British firms were actually expropriated, as they were in 1956, the prospect of such a happening had been fully discussed in the Calico board room.[61]

Textile overproduction was felt severely by SEIT, was commented on regularly by the Calico board, and was a major reason for the declining profitability of the SEIT enterprise.[62] Calico board member C. R. Hargreaves's report on a large expansion of the Egyptian textile industry in 1949 referred to the fact that the textile market was grossly overstocked and that industries were under state pressure to deal with the problem of unemployment.[63] SEIT's difficulties were only intensified when a gentlemen's agreement with Beida broke down. According to this tacit arrangement SEIT did not produce black cloth, which Beida specialized in, and Beida did not print. Beida's decision to install eight printing machines in 1949 as part of a general textile expansion freed SEIT to manufacture black cloth. But the Calico firm was far from sanguine about this more vigorous competition since Beida was known to be the more efficient producer.[64]

Thus by the early 1950s the Egyptian textile situation looked bleak to the Calico board. Linus Gasche was preparing to resign because of poor health. SEIT had a poor fiscal and trading year in 1952 and had incurred heavy losses. Yet the government kept pressuring firms to maintain high levels of production and a large labor force.[65] In Britain, Calico was now forced to use profits from its domestic operations and from the more profitable overseas affiliates to create a new reserve fund against losses in its overseas investments. This special reserve grew from £300,000 in 1953 to £600,000 in 1954 and £1 million in 1956.[66]

Could the Calico board lift SEIT from its decline? Virtually every proposal suggested by its members proved unworkable. Increasingly the SEIT situation compelled the board to recognize that the Egyptian investment had become one from which little good could come. In 1950 McCulloch, who had negotiated the first treaty, went back to reexamine the conditions of production at the plant. His report offered little optimism. While he conceded that the finishing processes at the SEIT plant were first-rate, he also admitted that the technical standard of the work was still not high. The SEIT factory could handle simple coloring and uniform designs, but its capability of producing more finely spun, higher quality cloth was severely limited. Since the highest profits came in these lines, McCulloch saw little chance that the company would become a strong revenue earner.[67]

Surplus production could be overcome through export. In this area SEIT and Filature struck a guarded note of optimism. In 1953 the Egyptian government created the Caisse de Consolidation to encourage exports. In 1954 SEIT and Filature together exported 650 tons or 5,856,904 square meters of cotton piece goods, worth LE 459,889, with Libya buying LE 226,426, the Sudan LE 160,780, Indonesia LE 36,957, and Gaza LE 22,091.[68] Nevertheless, in this area of promise SEIT and Filature were at a disadvantage to the Beida-Misr Fine Spinning and Weaving complex, which from its inception in the late 1930s had taken the dominant position in the finely spun, high quality cloth market.

The more radical alternative of selling off its shares in SEIT had great appeal to the Calico board, the more so as the Manchester directors worried about Egypt's political direction and concluded that SEIT could not be put on a sound financial and production footing. Their pursuit of a buyer led inevitably to Linus Gasche and Filature. But Gasche had no incentive. He already had firm managerial control of SEIT and did not contemplate expanding the company. Nonetheless Hargreaves initiated discussions with Gasche in Rome, only to learn that Gasche was not interested. The conversations were terminated.[69]

A final alternative did seem to offer an almost miraculous way out of Egypt. According to the original agreement creating SEIT, the charter of the company was to last for twenty years. Thus, in 1954, unless renewed, SEIT would come to an end. Its assets would be liquidated and divided among the three major shareholders. But even this option, which the Calico board favored, could not be realized. Calico was told that unless it renewed the charter the Egyptian government was likely to refuse to allow liquidation or would place heavy taxation on the distribution of reserves and accumulated profits.[70] While concluding that Calico had in fact been reduced to the status of little more "than that of an ordinary investor" in SEIT, the Calico board reluctantly and pessimistically agreed to a charter extension of thirty years.[71]

This extension was initialed in 1951. Five years later, following the British-French-Israeli invasion of Egypt, the British investment in SEIT was taken over by the Egyptian Economic Organization. Calico's shareholdings in Filature were sequestered.

The resolution of Calico's claims for compensation was the final disappointment for Calico. The British and Egyptian governments conducted prolonged and often acrimonious discussions over blocked assets. According to the agreement for the settlement of all outstanding claims, Calico holdings in SEIT, which the British Foreign Compensation Commission valued at LE 28 per share or LE 1,319,487 for Calico's 46,625 shares, were settled at about 30 percent of total value, LE 494,872.

When one considers that SEIT made profits of LE 2,749,021 between 1935 and 1954 from which the dividend payments to Calico totaled approximately LE 770,000, Calico's noncompounded return on nominal capital of approximately 23 percent per year was a handsome one, far in excess of ordinary British rates of return during these years. The interest rate on British consols, for example, fluctuated between 3 and 5 percent during this period. Even if one takes into account that Calico received only 30 percent of the share value of the firm at the time of compensation, the investment would still have compared favorably with most other alternative opportunities available to the Calico board. An additional lucrative aspect of SEIT for the Calico board members was the salaries paid to SEIT directors. (The ten directors received 10 percent of net profits after the payment of a 5 percent statutory reserve and a 5 percent dividend. During the mid-1940s, for instance, a Calico director's fee averaged LE 2,000 to LE 3,000 per year, a handsome stipend for little work.) Still, one must not lose sight of the fact that at a stroke the parent firm lost 70 percent of the value of a major affiliate.

Although Bradford Dyers experienced the same set of dilemmas in Egypt and ultimately faced the same result (expropriation), its post-war history was markedly different from Calico's. Beida Dyers demonstrated that Egyptian textiles could be profitable.

To an even greater extent than Calico, the Bradford financial recovery depended heavily on wartime orders and overseas investments. The severe arrears on the preference stock began to be alleviated in 1937; by 1942 these accounts had been cleared. In 1943 the regular preference dividend of 5 percent was paid, and a 4 percent dividend on ordinary stock was declared. From then onwards dividend payments on ordinary stock tended to be 5 percent of nominal capital, and the company once again began to set aside portions of its profits in reserve funds.[72]

The overseas investments lifted Bradford from its 1930s financial crisis. Although Bradford had restricted its overseas investment (more so than Calico), its interests were large ones and highly profitable. In 1948, for example, the parent company estimated its shareholding in subsidiaries at about £1.8 million out of total company assets of £6,378,642. It averred in its annual report for that year that these involvements were "well worth the amount at which [they] stand on the books".[73] In the same year the firm sold its interest in its textile plants in India and Ethiopia while retaining its Egyptian enterprise and expanding its commitments in the United States, Australia, and Canada. Bradford's Rhode Island plant was one of the largest commission dyeing and finishing works in the United States. With the acquisition of Consolidated Piece Dyers of Canada, which was then the largest commission wool dyers in Canada, the Bradford board could boast that the parent and affiliated companies were the largest cotton, rayon, and wool piece goods dyers in the world.

According to the 1948 report, "a substantial part of our profit comes from our foreign subsidiary companies and the association is now reaping the reward of its patient policy over many years in developing its activities in other countries."[74] In 1950 the foreign subsidiaries processed one third of the total yardage handled by Bradford.[75] Increasingly the Bradford dividend payments and accumulating reserves came from the profits of the affiliated companies. Of the £1,063,280 increase in gross trading profits in 1950, no less than three fifths was thanks to the overseas companies. Indeed, in that year Bradford paid out £353,000 in preference and ordinary dividends, of which £312,000 had been received in dividend payments from abroad. Of the £6.6 million in total company assets in 1951, £2.5 million were from the subsidiaries. The handsome dividend of 12.5 percent of that year (on nominal shares of £1 per share) was paid entirely from overseas profits. Only the debenture interest and the preference share dividends were charged against profits generated by the domestic company.[76]

An essential component of the lucrative Bradford empire was the Beida company in Egypt, which by 1945 had established itself as the premier finisher of high quality textiles in Egypt. Beida's decision to modernize and produce even those commodities which competed with Lancashire exports had proven a correct one. It had made the Egyptian enterprise far more profitable than its Calico competitor. Even more inspired was its alignment with the Misr complex, which overcame technical and managerial deficiencies through the size of its operations, access to capital, and influence with the government. The Beida shares at war's end, nominally valued at LE 4 per share, had risen to LE 30, and the original Bradford investment in Beida Dyers (LE 225,015) was then worth LE 1.5 million. Moreover, through the alliance between Beida and the Misr textile complex, particularly the Misr Spinning and Weaving Company at Mahalla, the Misr and Beida firms together controlled almost three quarters of cotton piece goods production, despite the efforts of competitors to wrest this market away from them.

These positive signs notwithstanding, Beida's future concerned the Bradford board. In 1945 T. C. Fisher, who kept surveillance over Egyptian matters, submitted a gloomy report. Questioning "whether the prospects of Beida justify [Bradford] in allowing such a large proportion of its total resources to be locked up in Egypt", Fisher worried about the rise of competitive textile industries in neighboring Arab countries. If successful, these firms would block an Egyptian export drive and might even invade the local market. He also anticipated a revival of Italian import competition and was exceedingly troubled by the possibility of "social upheavals and a change in Egyptian government policy in relation to protected industries". This prescient report concluded that "a danger of expropriation or penal taxation on foreign investment" existed. Fisher recommended a scaling down, if not an outright liquidation, of the Bradford interests in Egypt.[77]

Given the profitability of the Egyptian investment (which had already paid 100 percent returns on the original investment), it is doubtful that the home board would have withdrawn from the country at this juncture. Qualms were overcome, however, by a rising and brilliant employee and new manager of the Beida company, Elias Andraus, a Coptic Christian, who had been educated in the Sudan and had joined Beida in the accounting department. Through the sheer force of his personality, his understanding of men, and his sure grasp of Egyptian politics, rather than by virtue of any specialized textile expertise, he rose into the higher management ranks of the Egyptian firm. Already in 1945 he was on the board of Beida and was influential. He was destined to become chairman of the board and the controlling presence in Beida. His intelligently crafted report countered Fisher's arguments. Scoffing at the competition of other Arab industries on the grounds of their gross inefficiency, he forecast a great economic boom in the Egyptian economy and an accompanying huge demand for Egyptian textiles, largely from small Egyptian consumers who had not previously counted in the marketplace. The economic boom would overcome social problems and obviate the danger of expropriation. Nor would the state enact penal taxation on foreign investments. Andraus predicted "an extravagant return in dividend and/or bonuses" and expected the value of Bradford's investment to rise from LE 1.5 million to LE 3.5 million in five years' time.[78]

The parent firm accepted Andraus's vision and approved a substantial expansion of plant between 1945 and 1950. To begin with, Beida constructed a second factory, thus giving the firm increased output, without, however, any enhancement of technical capabilities. The expansion entailed a fateful decision. In approving the program the Bradford directors knowingly extinguished the last bit of market left to English producers and their merchants.[79] Shortly after the expansion, Beida installed a third factory in 1948, a printworks which took fabric from the main factories and returned the fabric for finishing.

These developments increased the importance and exposure of Bradford in Egypt. Yet Bradford, like Calico, allowed management control to slip from its hands. The rise of Andraus proved irresistible, and he became managing director upon Butterworth's retirement in 1947. Although talented and energetic, he had not risen within the Bradford milieu and was not committed to the larger Bradford goals. Bradford's failure to keep British managers in their Egyptian affiliate gave Andraus a free hand, for while the parent firm recognized the financial significance of Beida and while the home directors made occasional trips to Egypt, they were unable to persuade their better managers to serve there. Most of the high-management level British personnel who did go to Egypt did not stay long. The most forceful and knowledgeable textile individual to go to Egypt after World War II was Frank Sharples, who had served on the Bradford board for a number of years and was posted to Egypt during a difficult period of expansion. But even he was unable to arrest the loss of control over the Egyptian affiliate.[80]

Thus it was Andraus's vision which shaped the Egyptian company in the critical postwar years. Chairman Ewing alternately bemoaned the loss of control and asserted that Andraus had Bradford's interests at heart. In 1949, while conceding that Bradford had little authority in Beida, he argued that "to take part in control we require a strong man on the spot. Apart from Mr. Butterworth no one had proved to be one." When things went well, he claimed that the production side of things was in the hands of sound British technicians and that the main Bradford concern was "the maintenance of harmony in relations with the Misr company", which Andraus and the other Egyptian board members provided. "The interests of the Egyptian directors," he added, "were practically the same as ours, and it was reasonable to assume that in looking after their own interests they took care of ours."[81]

These rosy comments could be made in the bullish postwar aftermath. But as Egyptian industrialization, especially textile development, slowed, the Bradford board grew restive. Beida did not achieve Andraus's prediction of becoming a LE 3.5 million enterprise. The Yorkshire board was concerned about how to repatriate the large Beida profits and accumulated reserves without arousing nationalist resentment. Sharples was sent out in 1948 to increase the share capital by turning the large reserve funds into equity and bringing the shareholding value of the company into line with the company's intrinsic value. By increasing the share capital in this way Beida would be able to make larger dividend payments, which were at that time running as high as 37.5 percent of nominal capital. Sharples was also expected to develop proposals for arresting the decline in company profits.[82] And he was to check the ambitions of Andraus, whose schemes for expending reserves on new projects, like a caustic soda factory and a new textile plant in the Sudan, had not won the favor of the Yorkshire board.[83]

In 1953 the British element in Beida Dyers was able to reassert itself.[84] Andraus, having come under suspicion from the new military regime, had lost much of his political clout. He died in the same year,[85] and was succeeded as managing director by G. W. Bird, who had served with Beida Dyers in Egypt almost from its inception. The works manager, W. D. Fisher, had joined Beida in 1947 and now served on the board. Both were Bradford men, with their roots deep in Yorkshire and the parent company. Yet in spite of the fact that three Britons served on the Beida board and resided in Egypt, and that several other technicians were based there,[86] British control was precarious.

The number of Britons based in Egypt and working for Beida fluctuated a great deal over the two decades of the company's existence. It was, however, never a large contingent. At the outset approximately ten British managers worked in Egypt to get the plant established. Then during and just after World War II the decline of the British staff enabled the Egyptian element to rise. At the end, however, as Bradford was endeavoring to reestablish its control over Beida Dyers, the resident British contingent comprised three board members (G. W. Bird, K. Cranshaw and W. D. Fisher), an accountant (B. Blades), and about ten technical experts.

Beginning in 1949, and increasingly up to 1956, the Bradford board reopened the option of selling its Egyptian holdings. Although the rate of profit had declined (as had the share price—from LE 30 to LE 20 per share), Beida was still a prized asset. According to the British commercial attaché, reporting in 1955, it was the only well-run, thoroughly modern textile plant in the country.[87] In glaring contrast to SEIT, Beida had marketability; even more importantly, the Misr complex was interested in purchasing the Bradford shares and had the resources to do so. As part of a further expansion effort Bradford Dyers agreed to sell to the Misr Spinning and Weaving Company 80,000 shares of its total of 134,740, at LE 20 per share. Not wishing, however, to terminate its involvement in Egypt, although now willing to accept a minority managerial position, Bradford held on to 54,740 of its original shares and acquired an additional 54,700 at LE 4 per share (worth LE 218,800) in a new, expanded, and Misr-controlled Beida-Misr firm (equity capital of LE 2 million). In this company, not only would Bradford receive dividends out of the company's anticipated profits, but it would also be paid a fee for providing technical and managerial assistance.[88]

The new contract was signed in May 1956. At that point no one could dispute that Beida Dyers had been a highly profitable and wise investment. On a total capital investment of LE 540,000 (starting with LE 200,000 in 1938, with additions up to 1951) the company had received LE 1,366,578 in dividends and LE 1.6 million from the sale of 60 percent of its original shares. Moreover, at a time of heightened nationalist sensitivity in Egypt Bradford succeeded in making a favorable financial deal, which, had it not been for the British-French-Israeli invasion, would have enabled it to repatriate most of its equity capital. In the wake of the tripartite aggression the government Egyptianized the Bradford shares in Beida Dyers (estimated by the Foreign Compensation Commission in 1960 at LE 1,774,470), and sequestered Bradford's deposits with Bank Misr and the National Bank of Egypt, which together with interest to 1960 totaled LE 1,112,432.[89] Bradford received 33 percent of the total due it, leaving the company with a LE 1.3 million loss.

In spite of this final bad fortune, the Bradford investment in all other respects was a stunning success, especially compared with the Calico effort. The reasons for success are not hard to discern. First, the company had a better-trained technical staff, due in some measure to the cadre of British technicians serving in Egypt. Second, although the overseas managerial control had great gaps, Bradford exercised more surveillance than Calico. Some of its ex-directors served as directors on the Beida board. As befitted an investment of such magnitude, the Bradford directors included Egypt on their overseas tours of inspection and had a say in policy matters. But these were not the crucial reasons. The two most important factors were the original investment choices: the decision to establish an integrated fine-spinning textile complex, offering the highest quality production in Egypt; and the decision to align with the Misr Spinning and Weaving Company.

The May 1956 agreement between Beida and the Misr group seemed to mark a new departure for the textile industry of Egypt. For a long time textile experts had been arguing that it was folly to use expensive Egyptian cotton to manufacture articles of mass consumption. In 1956 the government concurred and approved the Misr plans to create a new textile combine, composed of the Misr Bank, the Misr Spinning and Weaving Company at Mahalla, Beida Dyers, Bradford Dyers Association, and the Misr Fine Spinning and Weaving Company. The plans called for the establishment of a vertically integrated spinning and weaving plant in the Suez Canal area, where Indian cotton would be used to produce cheap cloth, destined in the first instance for sale at home and later, if the plant proved viable, for export throughout the Middle East. By erecting this factory in the Suez area, the new company would not pose a disease threat to cotton cultivators in the Nile basin. The new company was to have a share capital of LE 2 million or LE 2.5 million, with each participant subscribing LE 400,000. The first plans envisaged 500 looms and 25,000 spindles (a small fraction of existing capacity), but also anticipated doubling the capacity. Implicit in the proposal was the expectation that the cotton factories in Cairo and Alexandria would specialize in fine spinning and weaving.[90]

The first stages of import-substitution industrialization proved to be relatively easy in Egypt. Once the local market for consumer products had been captured, a new stage of economic development was reached. Recent Third World experience suggests that countries at this threshold point which break into export markets fare better economically and even politically than those which attempt to widen the import-substitution market by protecting intermediate and capital goods industries. In Egypt an import-substitution crisis was reached in the 1950s. The consumer market for textiles and processed foods was saturated. Overt and disguised unemployment existed, and radical nationalist critics launched bitter attacks against the private sector. Unfortunately, Egypt's import-substitution industries did not exist on a secure economic footing. Their export prospects were poor. Because they produced an overpriced commodity in a poor country, their output per consumer was low. The government, desperate to facilitate industrial progress, opted in favor of extending the tariff barriers so as to protect new and technically more sophisticated industries, like iron and steel and chemicals. But before any of these departures could be brought to fruition, the Egyptian military dismantled the private sector and created a state-dominated economy.

The histories of these two British-affiliated textile firms in Egypt add further dimensions to our study of the impact of multinationals and direct foreign investment in a developing country. We are now in a position to evaluate the activities of Beida and SEIT in light of the issues raised in chapter 1. We have already dealt at length with the reasons for entering Egypt and the terms of entry (see chapter 2), so here we confine our remarks to the appropriateness of technology, the economic consequences, and the political, social, and cultural effects.

The technology introduced by the British firms lifted the textile industry of Egypt to a new stage of development. They imported expert finishing processes and the capability of producing more finely spun and expertly woven cloth. In general the textile technology of the 1930s was not extremely capital-intensive, and given the fact that all the modern firms in Egypt hired more workers per machine than was usual in western Europe and North America, the textile sector quickly became the largest employer of industrial labor. To be sure, the new factories spelled the end of Egypt's artisan spinning and weaving industry, already in sharp decline because of the import of cheap European, Indian, and Japanese textiles. The one complaint that could be made of the British firms is that their presence made it difficult for local entrepreneurs to enter the bleaching, dyeing, and printing end of the textile business. But in the 1930s there was no surge of indigenous business interest in textile finishing. All the interested local businessmen, including the economic nationalist, Tal'at Harb, looked to establish joint ventures with foreign firms. The British companies succeeded over competitors because they offered attractive terms.

Given the limited influence that Bradford and Calico had over their affiliates it is hardly surprising that their political impact was negligible. If anything, the firms recognized that they did not understand the Egyptian political situation, and because of the centrality of political decisions to the success of their business enterprises they believed it essential to align with well-placed and politically influential local firms. SEIT and Beida Dyers joined the Egyptian Federation of Industries and participated in the activities of the British Chamber of Commerce. But because neither firm had a large contingent of British personnel in Egypt, they were not active politically and allowed their affiliates or their Egyptian agents (Elias Andraus) to be the major political actors. Of Andraus's influence on politics, there can be no question. He was a man of enormous political energy. As head of Beida Dyers, he was enmeshed in the political arena. He had a reputation as a political manipulator, friend of King Faruq and ally of minority political parties. Beida Dyers gave him a platform from which to operate, but he did so autonomously from the parent firm.

There are occasional references in the Calico records to corruption as a feature of the Egyptian business and political environment. Some analysts of multinationals suggest that their political involvement is often corrupting. The Calico board discussed bribery when contemplating investment in Egypt. For its members peculation was a deterrent and worked against entry into the country or forced them into alignments with Egyptian businessmen and politicians better able to cope in the local political economy. There is no reason to believe that the Bradford and Calico participation in Egyptian affairs raised the level of corruption, already quite high. Indeed the contrary was probably the case, since the British textile men steered clear of politics.

Many foreign firms have also been excoriated for inculcating in people of the Third World preferences for products of Western manufacture of dubious value. They have been criticized for undermining the integrity and ethos of traditional societies by extolling the virtues of the material prosperity of the West and creating a largely unrealizable thirst for Western goods. What indeed is the value of sweetened and carbonated drinks or designer jeans to people struggling to achieve balanced diets and wear affordable clothing, the crities inquire? Foreign firms have also been accused of creating a consumer culture, modelled on the affluent lifestyles of the West, their primary weapon in this campaign being advertising and the mass media.

These complaints hardly seem applicable to the Bradford and Calico efforts in Egypt, not simply because the firms were involved in Egypt before the onslaught of the mass media but also because they did not engage in extensive advertising. The various kinds of cotton cloth produced in the Beida and SEIT factories were already in great demand in Egypt. There is no evidence that these firms made any effort to alter Egyptian preferences in cloth and clothing. The Beida Dyers factory was reassembled from an English plant which specialized in the manufacture of black cottons intended for export to the Middle East and sale to the women in that area. There was, of course, underway in Egypt as elsewhere in Asia and Africa a powerful movement in favor of wearing European-style clothing. But it would be difficult to contend that Beida or SEIT played anything but a marginal role in this cultural transformation. In their plants they were prepared to manufacture whatever the Egyptian consumers preferred to purchase.

Nonetheless, the main complaint against the foreign business presence is that it is a bad financial bargain for the host country. The profits, often described as excessive, are distributed to Western shareholders and swell the reserve funds of parent companies. To what extent, then, does this standard criticism fit he Calico and Bradford activities in Egypt?

In the first place the notion that the entry of Calico and Bradford into Egypt was exceedingly injurious to the Egyptian economy is hard to sustain. There is almost no evidence that local entrepreneurs would have entered the finishing trades in the 1930s. It seems clear that without foreign investment in this area there would have been no bleaching, dyeing, and printing of a sophisticated nature in Egypt until after World War II. But even had local finishing firms emerged there is no guarantee that the shareholders and directors of these companies would have kept their dividend payments inside the country. Frequently the wealthy indigenous classes prefer to invest their savings in what seem to them to be safer money markets in Western Europe and North America.

As for the actual financial performance of these companies, the returns were generally good to excellent. But were they exploitative, however one defines that term? Did they constitute a bad bargain for Egypt, the host country? Beida Dyers was a clear-cut financial success and was recognized as such by the parent firm. The Egyptian company paid three times as much in dividends between 1939 and 1956 as the parent firm invested in it. When one remembers that the original Bradford investment took the form of idled machinery, the return seems all the greater—in line with the dependency theorists' charge that overseas firms repatriate far more in profits than they invest. Nonetheless, this criticism must be tempered by the fact that Beida plowed back into the company's reserves a high proportion of its profits. Whereas total profits made by Beida Dyers up to 1956 were LE 3,070,000, the reserves in that year stood at LE 2,814,168.

In light of the criticisms often made about transfer pricing as a mechanism by which a multinational shifts capital and profits from one affiliate to another (usually, however, between countries) in order to maximize its return at the expense of competitor firms and host state, it is interesting to compare the profits of Beida Dyers with those of its local affiliates, the Misr Fine Spinning and Weaving Company and the Misr Spinning and Weaving Company. These two firms supplied Beida with yarn and woven cotton piece goods for finishing. The profits of Beida during the postwar decade (1945–46 to 1955–56) averaged 41.9 percent, or about the same as those of the Misr Spinning and Weaving Company (39.4 percent), but 10 percent less than those achieved by the Misr Fine Spinning and Weaving Company (51.5 percent). Moreover, the reserves of the Misr Fine Spinning and Weaving Company and the Misr Spinning and Weaving Company were respectively three and three and a half times as large as those of Beida Dyers. We have no information on pricing arrangements and thus cannot account for these variations. But it is true that the Misr firms had the controlling position in the integrated textile complex of which Beida was a component part. Bradford had no official of its own able to challenge the authority of the Misr textile managers. Elias Andraus was of course the leading Beida manager, but as the Bradford records indicate, he and Bradford valued a close and amicable, albeit subordinate, working relationship with the Misr firms.

Much the same picture emerges in the Filature-SEIT relationship. Unfortunately we do not have information on SEIT's dividends and reserves, but its profits as a proportion of its nominal capital were consistently less than those of its affiliate (28.4 percent vs. 40.5 percent). Filature provided much of the woven fabric for SEIT's finishing processes. As the managing director of both firms was Linus Gasche, and as he was virtually unchecked by any Calico official, he would have been in a position to price intermediate commodities (like yarn and woven fabrics) and the finished products so as to favor Filature at the expense of SEIT.

The underlying reality for Bradford and Calico in all their actions in Egypt was an inability to control the actions of their affiliates. By the standard and well-accepted definitions of multinational enterprises these two companies were multinationals. Yet the board minutes and letters from Egypt reveal just how misleading shareholding proportions and directorships can be. Despite Calico's owning 50 percent of SEIT, and Bradford more than half the shares of Beida Dyers, neither parent company had firm managerial control. In the operations of SEIT the key decisions were made by Linus Gasche, also managing director of Filature, the other parent firm. Calico never succeeded in dispatching one of its own directors to Egypt, and since board meetings and management decisions were made in Egypt, the British parent had been rendered powerless by the early 1950s.

Bradford Dyers did exercise greater control over its affiliate, but even so its inability to retain the services of good British directors in Egypt kept the home company from becoming dominant there. In time, Elias Andraus rose to become managing director. His intimate knowledge of the Beida operations and experience in the complicated world of Egyptian politics enabled him to supercede even hand-picked Bradford representatives sent out to reassert the power of the parent firm. Complaints, so frequent among Calico board members, about loss of authority, the independent actions of the managing director, and his failure to consult with the parent board, also abounded in the Bradford board discussions.

The case histories of these two firms serve as a reminder that sheer ownership percentages and even proportions of directors on the boards of companies do not provide decisive evidence about the locus of power. If a multinational is to control the operations of its affiliates and subsidiaries, it must be able to place its own men in the responsible positions. The parent firm must also have access to detailed information about developments in the subsidiary so that these problems can be discussed by the board of the parent company. In these important respects neither firm had developed into a full-fledged multinational. They were unable to dominate their Egyptian affiliates. The home boards were never well informed about policy questions being discussed on the spot. Often they learned about crucial issues after they had been resolved. Neither firm posted rising young men to overseas affiliates or used these companies as a proving ground for the home firm.

The control over foreign subsidiaries and affiliates can be a difficult matter and can require elaborate and carefully adhered-to procedures, as two counterexamples, also drawn from Egyptian-based business firms, will indicate. The first, the Suez Canal Company, was closely run from its headquarters in Paris. The board of the Canal Company in the 1940s and 1950s was an unwieldy body of thirty-two directors of various nationalities, mainly French and British. It met, nonetheless, once a month, usually only to discuss the most serious policy matters. The true locus of power and the brains of the company was the *Comité de Direction*, which consisted of nine directors including the president. This body dealt with all policy questions and even innumerable detailed issues. The company's principal representative in Egypt, the *Agent Supérieur*, was handpicked by the Paris board. Invariably a Frenchman, he had a strong commitment to the ethos of the parent company. The *Agent Supérieur* resided in Egypt and had day-to-day control over the operations of the company and its large staff.

The second example, the Anglo-Egyptian Oil Company, a subsidiary of Shell Oil, evolved different but equally effective mechanisms of control. Only the most general policy matters were ever referred back to the parent board in London, which had an extensive empire of oil affiliates to oversee. Instead, the board of Anglo-Egyptian Oil, based in Egypt and holding its annual meetings in Cairo, enjoyed virtually full management control. Even though most of the board members were drawn from the Egyptian business elite—and after World War II were Egyptian nationals—the fount of authority was the managing director, who resided in Egypt and was always a

Shell Oil man himself. He was certain to be a person groomed within the parent firm, who had risen through exemplary service in the overseas subsidiaries. This individual ensured that Anglo-Egyptian Oil's policies were compatible with those of the parent firm. Because the parent had such far-flung interests, it was rare for home directors, let alone the chairman of the board, to visit the country.

4

Foreign Capital in Egypt
in 1956

Although the textile industry had not become the dynamic sector which its apologists and government officials had intended it to be, it was hardly a cause for acute concern in the mid-1950s. It was still mobilizing substantial capital and providing employment for large numbers. Nor was the foreign presence excessive. If anything, British investment was trapped in Egypt, firmly under the control of men on the spot. More significantly, Egypt's textile firms were attempting to overcome their production difficulties by creating a large combine in the Suez Canal zone where cheap, imported raw cotton would finally be used to manufacture textiles for the home market (and ultimately for export to the Middle East and Africa). The older factories in Cairo, Alexandria, and the Delta could then be upgraded to enable them to produce expensively fashioned, high count textiles for which Egyptian cotton gave the country an obvious advantage. It was not unreasonable to assume that Egyptian textile firms in the Delta could compete in world markets. In all these projections much was expected from the British companies. In the upgrading of the Cairo, Alexandria, and Delta factories, the Beida factory was likely to serve as a model. In the Canal zone Beida and Bradford were counted on to make important capital and technical contributions.

Yet on November 1, 1956, the Egyptian government sequestered British and French holdings in Egypt, including the Bradford and Calico assets. From one vantage point this action was far from unexpected, not only because it followed the British-French-Israeli invasion of Egypt, but because threats (and even in some cases actual use) of economic boycotts and sequestrations had marked the strained Anglo-Egyptian relations in the decade after World War II. But this time most of the companies and properties were not desequestrated and returned to their original owners. They were in fact nationalized and turned over to a newly created state body, the Economic Organization. Subsequently in 1960 and 1961 the assault on foreign capital was made complete when the Egyptian government also nationalized Belgian business holdings.

In light of the Bradford and Calico record in Egypt—their palpable contributions to textile development and their anticipated role in the large expansion of textile production contemplated by the state and the business community—how do we account for the nationalization of the Bradford and Calico investments? More significantly, how do we explain the dissolution of the entire large-scale private foreign sector between 1956 and 1961? Perhaps British investment in textiles was not typical of other types of foreign investment in the Egyptian economy—an aberration wherein Egypt had gained mastery over foreign capital because of Lancashire's weaknesses. Or did much of the foreign investment in the 1940s and 1950s resemble Bradford's and Calico's involvement? If the latter was the case, then explanations for the nationalization of foreign enterprises are likely to be located outside the economic sphere, in the realm of ideology and elsewhere. (There is agreement among observers that the Nasser government had an uncertain grasp of economics and that its perception of foreign capital — that it was omnipresent, overweening, grossly exploitative, and threatening to Egyptian sovereignty — was drawn from the officers' experiences in the 1930s rather than the circumstances of the 1950s.[1])

Answering these questions requires a broadening of the scope of the inquiry. We will need to examine foreign capital in other sectors of the economy, in particular in banking, oil production, public utilities, and the Suez Canal Company, where foreign capital had always reigned supreme. Once again the focus will be the firms themselves rather than highly aggregated industry-wide statistics. While this approach may seem anecdotal and selective, it allows a deeper penetration into firm behavior.

By the 1950s, at the risk of oversimplifying, there were two main types of foreign firms in Egypt, both of which were coming under Egyptian mastery. The first resembled the Bradford and Calico firms. Although the foreign investors had considerable foreign managerial and technical involvement, they were unable to translate their influence into domination. Increasingly these firms were run on the spot and were not carefully supervised from Europe.

The second type, more visible and more likely to arouse nationalist scrutiny, was carefully linked to its European corporate and individual investors. Many of these firms were outright subsidiaries of multinationals (Anglo-Egyptian Oil), branches of foreign firms (Barclays Bank, DCO), and individual firms managed closely from Europe (the Suez Canal Company). Their much tighter relationship with overseas capital made it impossible for local business leaders to achieve managerial control. Yet through legislation and through the pressures exerted by Egyptian nationalist organizations even these companies were bent to the goals of the Egyptian economy. By

1955 none of these companies enjoyed the free-wheeling economic independence which had characterized their earlier behavior. They were mindful of Egypt's political and economic goals and were aware that a failure to produce desired results could lead to dire consequences.

The Loosely Administered Companies

In the companies resembling Beida and SEIT, capital flowing from Europe did not automatically bring managerial control. By the 1950s individuals and groups based in Egypt were running many firms registered in London, Paris, and Brussels, and financed by European investors. To a substantial extent the lack of clear-cut overseas managerial control stemmed from the diverse national sources of capital and from the ease with which new investment groups, even Egyptian elements, could acquire substantial blocks of stock. Most Egyptian firms even in the mid-twentieth century were not massively capitalized, nor were they closely integrated into multinational business empires. Through acquiring shares, even quite small blocks of shares and even in some cases bonds, the new investors could influence the operations of the company, especially if these shareholders were based in Egypt and were well informed about company finances.

A distinction is often made in the literature dealing with multinationals between direct and portfolio investment. Direct investment is said to entail administrative control; portfolio investment does not. Given the fluid nature of European investment in Egypt and the difficulty that European groups had in bringing their shareholding powers to bear on the management of companies in Egypt, it is not surprising that this distinction was often blurred. At certain moments and under certain management teams European concerns exercised direct control. But as the balance of financial power changed, direct control diminished. Overseas firms often ended up having only a portfolio interest in their Egyptian affiliates.

A look at the historical record of three large firms (the Egyptian Salt and Soda Company, Crédit Foncier Égyptien, and the Egyptian Sugar Company) may illustrate these patterns. The Egyptian press and subsequent scholarly works have regarded these companies as foreign and believed that they exercised a powerful influence in the Egyptian economy. A close examination reveals that local influence was important, even from the earliest days, and that Egyptian shareholding and management power grew steadily in the twentieth century.

The Egyptian Salt and Soda Company was incorporated in Britain in 1899 in order to attract British investors and to enable it to exploit concessions made to it by the government of Egypt for the manufacture and sale of salt in Egypt.[2] Its stock was sold on the London and the Egyptian Stock Exchanges. Apparently much of the stock was traded in Egypt. Companies like the Egyptian Salt and Soda Company were registered in London because British company law was less rigid than Egyptian law, particularly in fixing no minimum valuation on shares. In Egypt the smallest share permitted was LE 4, a restriction which made it difficult to attract small investors.[3]

The capitalization and functions of the Egyptian Salt and Soda Company grew steadily in the twentieth century. By the outbreak of World War II the firm had a nominal and paid-up capital of slightly over £600,000. It raised its capital to LE 1,260,000 by the end of the war, thus making it one of the most heavily capitalized industrial companies in Egypt at the time. By 1956 its capital stood at LE 1,413,618. Not only was the Egyptian Salt and Soda Company the largest salt producer and distributor in Egypt, but it also crushed oleaginous seeds, produced caustic soda, and manufactured oil cakes and soap.

As the company grew, it also became more Egyptianized. We do not know how many of its original investors were Egyptian or based in Egypt and how many were foreigners, but during World War II, when it requested permission from the British Treasury Capital Issues Committee to increase its capital, it submitted a report on the proportion of British and Egyptian shareholders. Of the total nominal capital of £600,000 only about £55,000 was held in the United Kingdom.[4] Moreover, all the directors of the company were resident in Egypt and all company board meetings were convened in Alexandria. At the time the chairman of the board was Alfred Lian, a British national resident in Egypt, and the general manager was G. Psacharopoulo, a Greek, but Egyptians were well represented on the board: Husayn Fahmi served as managing director, and 'Ali Amin Yahya, Hafiz 'Afifi, Isma'il 'Sidqi, and Aslan Qattawi were directors. The increase in capitalization which the Capital Issues Committee agreed to was achieved almost entirely through Egyptian participation, for in 1949 of the 1,058,090 total shares of the company, only 56,095 were held in the United Kingdom.[5] The overwhelming majority of the rest were held in Egypt. Finally, in April 1956 the Egyptian Salt and Soda Company turned itself formally into an Egyptian joint stock company.[6]

There were numerous other firms registered in the United Kingdom in which the financing and management were overwhelmingly Egyptian. Only 6,799 shares out of 488,736 shares of the Egyptian Hotels Limited, also established at the turn of the century, were held in the United Kingdom in 1946, and the board included among its directors such well-known local businessmen as Leon Castro and Joseph Kfouri. The chairman of the board was Baron Edouard Empain, the noted Belgian entrepreneur.[7] The same situation prevailed in the Egyptian Delta Land and Investment Company, a British firm with 480,275 bearer and regular shares, of which only 14,523 were held by persons resident in the United Kingdom.[8] These firms had been established in Britain to take advantage of British company law and to draw upon British investment capital. But since the companies themselves did business exclusively in Egypt and also traded on the Cairo bourse (which became increasingly active in the course of the twentieth century), investors in Egypt acquired large blocks of these holdings. By the end of World War II investors resident in Egypt had turned their shareholding predominance into managerial authority, albeit power wielded largely by foreign businessmen living in Egypt.

The Crédit Foncier Égyptien, along with the Suez Canal Company, was thought to be the linchpin of the French economic empire in Egypt. At the turn of the century it was the most heavily capitalized French firm in the country. Although the Crédit Foncier Égyptien was modeled after the Crédit Foncier de France, a French land mortgage company which provided financing and technical and managerial assistance to the Egyptian firm, the whole history of the Crédit Foncier Égyptien reveals how critically important local factors were in its corporate evolution.

The original inspiration for the Crédit Foncier Égyptien came from a local businessman, Raphael Suares, whose influence on nearly all the major business enterprises in this era was monumental.[9] Suares grouped around him other influential local businessmen from Cairo and Alexandria— Sinadino, Salvago, and Qattawi—and then approached Baron de Soubeyran of the Crédit Foncier de France with a proposal to establish a land mortgage company in Egypt. At the time the Suares family had close ties with European banking and financial houses and had little trouble in also interesting the Société Générale and the Crédit Lyonnais in the project. Subsequently the Banque de Paris et des Pays-Bas and the Maison Cohen d'Anvers also served as bankers to the Crédit Foncier Égyptien.[10]

When it was founded in 1880, with a capital of Fr 200 million the company enjoyed the financial backing of these powerful French groups. But local influence was, if anything, stronger, and destined to grow with the passing of time. In the decade before World War I the French consul in Cairo reported that, though French capital was in the majority, French influence on the board was minimal.[11] Only through French diplomatic intervention was a Frenchman, Miriel, made director-general of the firm in 1908. Miriel remained as head of the firm until his resignation in 1931, and during this period he was acknowledged as the head of the French business community in Egypt. Not only did he preside over the Crédit Foncier Égyptien, but he was a director of the Suez Canal Company, the Egyptian Sugar Company, and the Bank of Abyssinia—all businesses in which French capital was heavily involved. Following Miriel's resignation, the French Embassy once again intervened to secure a French successor, Marcel Vincenot, who served in this post until the 1950s.[12]

While the French Embassy ensured the selection of a Frenchman as chairman of the board, it was not able to block the rise of Egyptian financial and managerial power. Shares of the firm were traded on European and Egyptian bourses. Moreover, French shareholders with small and widely dispersed holdings were notoriously uninterested in management issues. Already by the 1930s Egyptians held a majority of the shares voted at board meetings (104,274 out of 201,123 voted in 1934; the French were represented by 82,259 votes).[13] According to the French ambassador French shareholders were still in the majority, estimated to hold between 225,000 and 250,000 out of the total 400,000 shares. Nonetheless, the Egyptian challenge was determined and effective. The Egyptian government commissioned Tal'at Harb, head of Bank Misr, to buy shares on its behalf. By 1935 Tal'at Harb had purchased 30,000 shares and had become the largest single shareholder.[14] Egyptians, as a consequence, won an important place on the board of Crédit Foncier Égyptien. Tal'at Harb served as one of its directors until his resignation from Bank Misr in 1939. Subsequently the Egyptian capitalist element was always well represented on the board. In 1953 the Crédit Foncier Égyptien had 'Ali Mahir, Muhammad Khalil, Hafiz 'Afifi, Mahmud Shukri, Husayn Sirri, and Rene Qattawi serving as directors.[15]

The important role played on the periphery of foreign investment by local businessmen is further illustrated by the foundation and early development of the Egyptian Sugar Company. This industry owed its beginning to Khedive Isma'il, who, wishing to end Egypt's dependence on a single agricultural export, encouraged the cultivation of sugar on royal and private estates in Upper Egypt and founded a number of sugar workshops. Like so many of Isma'il's projects, the sugar program foundered because of the government's financial distress.[16] Much of the emerging sugar industry found its way into private hands. Here, too, the Suares family played a decisive role. Just how strong the impulse from the periphery was can be seen from the fact that in the new sugar company established in 1893 by Suares and Company and a group of Cairene bankers, Suares subscribed 4,000 of the 6,000 shares. The remaining 2,000 were taken up by Ernest Cronier, a sugar engineer acting on behalf of the Say Refinery Company.[17]

As the capital of the Sugar Company increased so did the proportion of French shareholding. But French shareholding did not translate into clear

French managerial control. In 1897 the Sucrerie Raffinerie d'Égypte and the Société Générale des Sucreries de la Haute Égypte merged to form the Société Générale des Sucreries et de la Raffinerie d'Égypte, destined to be the dominant force in this industry. Shortly thereafter, an Anglo-Egyptian group, led by the British financier, Ernest Cassel, became major creditors of the firm.[18] The company's substantial indebtedness, coupled with mismanagement and overproduction, brought it to the verge of bankruptcy in 1905, and Cronier committed suicide.[19] Only because of the efforts of a locally-based business team of Henri Naus, a Belgian sugar expert, and Victor Harari was the company rescued from collapse.[20] Inevitably control slipped from the hands of the overseas investors. Although the Company had a Parisian advisory board to represent the interests of its French shareholders, this body's powers were severely circumscribed. The real locus of authority lay with the management board in Egypt, where power was dispersed among Naus, the Say representative, the representatives of the original Suares group, and even the Anglo-Egyptian team of Cassel and others.[21]

Naus piloted the company for more than three decades, during which period the Sugar Company grew into a profitable and well-administered enterprise. Large profits were made during World War I, and an accord signed with the state in 1931 reserved the local market to the firm and guaranteed it a five percent return on nominal capital. With the passage of time the influence of the Anglo-Egyptian creditors diminished, and their claims on the company were completely extinguished in the 1920s. Indeed, as long as Naus ran the firm, problems did not arise between shareholders and management. But Naus's death in 1938 raised difficulties, revealing in stark terms how little influence shareholders actually had over the running of the company. Again the French Embassy intervened, regarding the Sugar Company as an important French economic asset, yet aware that the management of the company had slipped into Belgian, Egyptian, and Greek hands. While the French held 96,000 out of the 348,000 shares (or 30 percent), less than 1 percent of the French holders were represented at shareholder meetings. A concerted effort on the part of Crédit Lyonnais to alert the French shareholders yielded only 5,640 French votes for the 1939 meeting, or about 6 percent of the total French shareholding voting power.[22]

By the 1930s control over the Sugar Company had slipped from French hands into those of a Greek contingent assembled around the Cozzika family. The Cozzikas held 75,000 shares and were influential in board meetings.[23] But Greek influence proved shortlived. The rising new star in the Egyptian business firmament, Ahmad 'Abbud, ultimately succeeded in taking over the direction of the company. His purchase of company shares, depressed during the 1930s, enabled him to enter the board in the early 1940s and also immediately to become its managing director. No doubt 'Abbud's elevation also stemmed from the company's desire to have as managing director an invididual well connected with the political elite. The company's economic fate depended heavily on its relationship with the state.

Although the French Embassy and business world still regarded the Sugar Company as a French economic asset, French shareholding continued to decline. In 1955 when the company was sequestered as a result of 'Abbud's dispute with the Egyptian government over taxes and pricing policy, French shareholding had declined to 80,000 out of 348,000 (or 26 percent). When the company was liquidated in May 1956 the government of Egypt reported that only 17 percent of the shares were still held in France.[24]

These are but three examples of foreign investment in the Egyptian economy—far from the full story, of course, yet similar in many respects to the Bradford and Calico experiences. Their evolution documents a familiar pattern for twentieth-century Egyptian corporate development. Capital was raised in Egypt as well as overseas. Egyptian business groups, mainly emerging from the foreign communities residing in Egypt, were quick to perceive new investment opportunities, much as the Egyptian textile merchants did for Calico and Bradford. These men and their backers were invariably represented on the boards of the new companies. One might want to call people like Suares, Harari, and 'Abbud comprador businessmen, for they played a critical role in integrating the Egyptian economy into the world economy. Certainly the Suares family and Harari spurred the spread of cotton cultivation and export through their support for land mortgage companies, banks, land development companies, and hydraulic reform. But their purview was not limited to the agricultural and export sectors. The Egyptian Salt and Soda Company and the Sugar Company, as industrial firms, led the drive to diversify the Egyptian economy. Compradors these men and others may have been, but they were far from the passive and dependent creations of European capitalism depicted in many studies. They were themselves the founders of new firms, and often they mobilized more than half the original share capital. With the passage of time the Egyptian shareholding and management element grew in each one of these undertakings. Just as in the cases of Calico and Bradford, European capital could be manipulated by shrewd local businessmen and was not subject to careful overseas control.

It would be difficult to argue that these companies were true multinational enterprises, although two of them (Crédit Foncier Égyptien and the Egyptian Sugar Company) had some of the features of multinationals. The Egyptian Salt and Soda Company was an Egyptian joint stock company, despite its being registered in England. The Crédit Foncier Égyptien and the Sugar Company possessed capital from French firms (Say Refinery, Crédit Foncier de France, and Société Générale), drew on the experience and technical know-how of these firms, and even employed some of their personnel. But their financial and administrative affiliation was loose.

Much more comparable to the model of the mid-twentieth-century multinational, with unequivocal overseas control, were the Belgian enterprises established in Egypt, notably those created by Baron Edouard Empain and the Banque Belge et Internationale en Égypte. Even here, however, overseas authority was insecure and even at times challenged in Egypt. Belgian capital was more centralized than British or French capital. A variety of huge conglomerates, like the Société Générale and the Bank of Brussels dominated the corporate structure, while overseas firms specialized in mining, railways, and tramways.[25] The most powerful of the holding companies, the Société Générale de Belgique, had a portfolio of public funds and companies in 1895 worth nearly half the assets held by all Belgian credit organizations.[26]

In Egypt the most visible Belgian entrepreneur was Baron Edouard Empain, creator of the Paris Metro and builder of tram and railways networks in France and the Netherlands. His most successful Egyptian achievement was the Cairo residential suburb of Heliopolis, brought into existence by his Cairo Electric Railways and Heliopolis Oases Company. We can probably consider the Empain group of companies as a precursor of multinational corporations, for these companies, though located in all corners of the globe, were centrally regulated from Brussels and Paris. Empain supported Leopold's imperialism in the Congo and ran companies or had investments in Russia, Spain, and China. But the Empain group, at least while Edouard was still alive, was more a prodigious one-man show than a vast bureaucratic business empire. It relied on the energy and business acumen of this single individual. Nor was it as tightly run and financed as later multinational enterprises. The individual Empain companies—Banque Empain, Compagnie des Tramways à Voie Étroite, and Compagnie des Chemins de Fer Réussis, to name but a few—had to raise their money separately and permitted the active participation of other powerful financial groups.[27] The Cairo Electric Railway and Heliopolis Oases Company, for instance, had at the outset 60,000 shares subscribed by twenty-two different organizations and individuals, including Banque de Paris et des Pays-Bas, Banque de Bruxelles, Tramways du Caire, and Société Générale de Chemins de Fer Économiques.[28] With such diverse and influential investors the Empain companies could not enjoy complete financial and managerial freedom.

These individual business histories point to a growing Egyptian shareholding and managerial presence. So do the broader statistical studies. Unfortunately none of these works is as definite as Crouchley's *Investment of Foreign Capital in Egypt,* published in 1936. The work of Abdallah Fikri Abaza, an undersecretary in the Ministry of Commerce and Industry, who had access to confidential corporate reports, has considerable merit, however. In extending Crouchley's data to 1948, Abaza documented the drift toward Egyptian equity participation. He found that 80 percent of the LE 26,457,000 shares of new stock companies created between 1934 and 1948 were subscribed in Egypt (see table 4.1). Extrapolating from these figures and the work done by Crouchley, he estimated that Egyptians held 39 percent of the total shares of joint stock companies in 1948, up from the 9 percent of 1914. The proportions of foreign and Egyptian shareholding must be regarded with caution. however. since many of the Egyptian-held shares were owned by Egyptian joint stock companies and did not belong to individual Egyptians. As for the foreign holdings, undoubtedly a high proportion belonged to the foreign community resident in Egypt. Through stringent legal regulations on the source of capital and the proportion of Egyptian directors and employees as required in the Company Law of 1947, and through the purchase of stock in the open market, many firms had become greatly Egyptianized in the ten years after World War II.

These firms, then, tended to be quite representative of foreign capital in Egypt; but they were not the most visible or the most tightly controlled from Europe. Nor were they the object of intensive nationalist scrutiny and suspicion. That unenviable position lay with the foreign banks, the oil conglomerates, the public utility concessionaires, and most assuredly, the Suez Canal Company. Because of financial size, reputed earning power, domination of key sectors of the local economy, control from Europe, and contact with numerous Egyptians, these firms had an intense, ambiguous, and frequently tumultuous relationship with the Egyptian state and the Egyptian populace. Was it then their visibility and extraordinary financial and political power which prompted the Egyptian political leaders to nationalize foreign businesses?

The Tightly Controlled Companies

Foreign banks, oil companies, and the Suez Canal Company represented those foreign corporations which were securely regulated from their corporate headquarters in Europe. They were unlikely to slip into Egyptian hands. Certain of these firms, most notably Anglo-Egyptian Oil and the Suez Canal Company, had always symbolized an overarching and exploitative foreign economic presence to Egyptian nationalists. Yet in the decade after World War II Egyptian politicians, spurred on by radical nationalism, took legislative steps to curb the independence of these firms.

Egypt's pre-1956 banking structure was overwhelmingly dominated by foreign concerns. The major land mortgage banks, although their influence diminished as the Egyptian economy became more diverse, retained strong European ties. The omnipresent and powerful commercial banks were either branch banks of European parent firms (Crédit Lyonnais, Crédit Nationale d'Escompte, and Barclays Bank, DCO) or independent Egyptian banks aligned tightly with overseas capital (Banque Belge et Internationale en Égypte, a spin-off of Banque Belge Etrangère and an affiliate of the Société Générale de Belgique). The only wholly Egyptian bank was Bank Misr, created in 1920 by Tal'at Harb and allowing only Egyptian shareholders and directors. The National Bank of Egypt, the institution most approximating a central bank, was primarily British-controlled, having come into existence in 1898 through the planning of Ernest Cassel and Lord Cromer. Most of its shareholders were foreign. Its governor until World War II was a leading British financial figure, and it maintained close ties with the Bank of England through its London-based consultative committee.

Barclays Bank, DCO was typical of the private foreign commercial banks operating in Egypt. It was the brainchild of F. C. Goodenough, chairman of Barclays Bank Ltd., who wrote in 1916: "In the coming struggle for the markets of the world the manufacturers of Great Britain will look to their bankers to assist them to a greater extent than hitherto."[29] As part of Goodenough's desire to create an international presence for Barclays, he aligned with the Colonial Bank in 1917, with a West Indian firm and the National Bank of South Africa in 1919, and with the Anglo-Egyptian Bank in 1925. Finally, the whole amalgam was consolidated into Barclays Bank, Dominion, Colonial, and Overseas in 1925, with an authorized capital of £10 million. In 1944 its issued capital was £4,975,500, its reserves £1.4 million, and its deposits £282,175,976. It was backed by the financial might of Barclays Bank Ltd., which in 1944 had an issued capital of £15,858,217, reserves of £11.25 million, and deposits totaling £917,775,560.[30]

Egypt was an important investment area for Barclays, said to involve 5 percent of the firm's world-wide business in the 1950s.[31] The bank played a large role in financing the cotton crop. During and following World War II its deposit banking expanded dramatically. The Cairo branch at the beginning of the war had only 5,600 accounts, but it opened 67,000 new accounts during the war.[32] At the time of its nationalization Barclays in Egypt had credits worth £38.75 million, represented by advances of £16.75 million, Egyptian treasury bills of £7.5 million, Egyptian government stocks of £3.75 million, and cash worth £8 million. It had forty-five offices located all over Egypt and a staff of 1,630, of whom twenty-seven were British.[33] The bank took immense pride in serving as paymaster of the British forces of occupation in Egypt and was prepared, as Foreign Office records indicate, to circumvent Egyptian regulations in order to make money available to the British forces during crises in Egyptian-British relations. There can be little question that Barclays Bank was a powerful force in the Egyptian economy even as late as the 1950s.

Nationalist criticism and even at times outrage at the foreign banking presence was a constant theme in Egyptian politics, dating back into the nineteenth century and coming to the fore during downturns in the world economy. It was on such occasions that leading Egyptian nationalist figures, many of them wealthy landlords with large lines of credit from these foreign banks, made their most insistent demands for their regulation and for the creation of indigenous banks more in tune with the needs of Egypt and less beholden to overseas shareholders and directors. Not surprisingly in 1956 the Egyptian government nationalized all these foreign firms. In 1957 it passed a law stipulating that all commercial banks must be Egyptian joint stock companies, possessing nominal shares, owned exclusively by Egyptian nationals.[34]

Yet even before 1956 the Egyptian government had taken steps to circumscribe the powers of the foreign banks, many of which were forced by legislation and common sense to be responsive to Egyptian concerns. The Egyptian government asserted its control first by bringing the National Bank of Egypt under state regulation in the late 1930s and 1940s and then using the powers of this quasi-central bank to control the private banking sector. A first step occurred in 1939 when the shareholders accepted an agreement that the majority of the board would be Egyptians, that Edward Cook's successor as governor of the bank would also be an Egyptian, and that the London Advisory Board would be done away with.[35] These changes aroused the opposition of a group of shareholders, mainly foreigners resident in Egypt (Cozzika, Sursock, Stagni, Choremi, Benachi, Aristophon, Adda, and Mallison, whose shares totaled 40,000 out of 300,000). Their opposition was led by Bertram Hornsby, a former governor of the bank and a present director.[36] But Cook overcame the complaints, pointing out that while two thirds of the shareholders did indeed live in Europe, no government could allow the majority of a board of a national bank to be foreigners and resident overseas.[37]

Perhaps Cook and Hornsby exaggerated the number of foreign investors, for by 1950, two years after shareholding had been made nominal, Egyptians had already achieved a plurality of the shares—74,422 out of

300,000 or 25 percent. British shareholding had declined to fourth place by that date (13 percent) behind the French (23 percent) and the Greeks (17 percent).[38]

The Egyptianization effort in 1939 initiated the evolution of the National Bank of Egypt into a central bank, and was followed by measures intended to increase its powers to regulate the money supply and to hold the deposits of the government and other banks. First, through a tacit agreement and then by legislation all private commercial banks were required to keep a proportion of their reserves with the National Bank. Egypt's withdrawal from the sterling monetary system in 1947 further enhanced the powers of the National Bank over the rest of the banking system. Through exchange controls and a more independent monetary policy the National Bank regulated the flow of funds in and out of the country as well as the availability of credit inside the country.[39]

To be sure, foreign banks still enjoyed considerable autonomy and wideranging financial strength on the eve of their nationalization. Although their share capital was only LE 5.2 million, their deposits totaled more than LE 100 million, roughly 50 percent of the total deposits of all commercial banks operating in Egypt. They still looked to their European parent firms for their financial cues, and they still provided most of the financing for the cotton crop.[40]

Besides the banks, the other important multinationals with a long history in Egypt included the oil conglomerates.[41] Egypt's early experience with these firms was far from successful, and since these companies supplied the country with vital oil products, their behavior contributed to Egyptian suspicion of foreign companies. Yet here, too, the state was able to gain the upper hand in the 1950s.

Two oil firms dominated the exploration, processing, and distribution of oil and oil products in Egypt: Anglo-Egyptian Oil and Socony-Vacuum. Anglo-Egyptian Oil was the first to enter Egypt and by far the more influential. The company owed its predominance to a concession granted just before World War I by Lord Kitchener, at the time Britain's consul-general in the country. Kitchener was eager to solidify Britain's control over the development of Egypt's oil resources. At the outset the firm had an issued capital of £676,000, which was increased to £1,808,000 in 1920.[42] The Egyptian government held £100,000 of these shares and was entitled to a seat on the board. Anglo-Egyptian Oil was a subsidiary of the Royal Dutch-Shell Oil group, although, like many oil affiliates, parental control was exercised through other affiliates. In this case Anglo-Saxon Petroleum held 34 percent and Anglo-Iranian Oil another 34 percent of non-government shares, but since both firms were subsidiaries of the Royal Dutch-Shell group parental oversight was unchallenged. Even though Egyptians owned 17 percent of the remaining stock in 1948, they constituted no threat to Royal Dutch-Shell Oil's preeminence.[43]

With considerable British assistance Anglo-Egyptian Oil assumed a primary position in Egypt's oil production and marketing. Not only did the firm produce two thirds of the total oil output from Egypt's wells, but through its large refinery at Suez and its well-developed marketing networks it dominated the distribution of oil products in Egypt. Marketing was handled by Shell Oil of Egypt, also a subsidiary of the overseas parent.

Egypt was a significant production area for the parent firm from the 1920s until 1956. While its output was only 3 percent of Shell's world production, Egypt was the fifth largest producing country for Shell behind Venezuela, the United States, British Borneo, and Indonesia.[44] The overseas conglomerate, as revealed in the first unified balance sheet of 1950, was a true international financial giant. Its world-wide resources were estimated at between £500 and £600 million and its net operating annual income totaled £200 million in 1950.[45]

The only competitor for Anglo-Egyptian Oil proved to be an American firm, Socony-Vacuum, which entered Egypt in the interwar years, also as a producer and distributor of oil products.[46] Socony was more a partner of Anglo-Egyptian Oil, however, than a competitor; these two firms worked in tandem to set prices and to present a united front to the Egyptian government.

Oil was an essential commodity within the Egyptian economy, especially as its popularity grew vis-à-vis coal as a fuel for use in Egyptian industries, railways, and trucking. In 1955 Egypt used 3,714,000 metric tons of petroleum products, compared with 432,260 in 1933. In the meantime coal imports had fallen from 1,130,733 metric tons in 1933 to 142,630 in 1954.[47] Kerosene was the most highly prized oil product for the mass of the population. Because of its relative cheapness and abundance people used it for cooking, fuel, heat, and light. Yet the local oil companies satisfied only 30 percent of the Egyptian demand, the rest having to be purchased on the world market.[48] Foreign oil producers and distributors came into contact with all segments of Egyptian society, from local industrialist to urban worker and peasant. The prices they set for the various types and grades of petroleum products had an immediate impact on everyone's cost of living. Not surprisingly the relationship between the state and the oil producers was frequently a troubled one.

In the interwar period the oil companies used their monopolistic position to gain the upper hand over the state. According to the original concession, Anglo-Egyptian Oil would supply government agencies with the oil products they required at cost. Yet in violation of this agreement it sold high-priced Egyptian *mazout* abroad and imported cheaper foreign *mazout* into Egypt, without paying customs, for sale in the country. When the Egyptian government asked for the right to inspect the Anglo-Egyptian Oil refinery, the company objected on the grounds that the processes used there were secret. Subsequently the government discovered that the refining processes were well known, fully described in a standard textbook. The company had used this argument to thwart the state's efforts to enforce the original agreement and by doing so had made illegal profits.[49]

These problems became more serious and the relationship more troubled in the 1930s. The downturn in the world economy was not accompanied by comparable reductions in the price of many oil products sold in the Egyptian markets. Egypt's efforts, particularly those engineered by Ahmad 'Abd al-Wahhab as Minister of Finance in the 1930s, to break the oil monopoly and to create real competition were largely without effect. 'Abd al-Wahhab brought in new oil prospectors and distributors, founded an Egyptian National Oil Company for production and distribution, imported oil from the world market, and expanded the small state-run Egyptian refinery. Yet by temporary price cutting, by inclusion of new firms in the pricing group, and by altering production lines to maximize profits, the foreign oil conglomerates withstood 'Abd al-Wahhab's challenge.[50] They emerged from the interwar period as strong and as unified as they had been at the outset.

Yet in the post-World War II era the government of Egypt was able to acquire the kind of control over this industry which had eluded it in the previous two decades. The enhancement of state authority stemmed in the first instance from a mining law passed by the Egyptian parliament in 1948, stipulating that mining leases, including new concessions for oil exploration, could be granted only to registered Egyptian companies. Since the Egyptian Company Law of 1947 required Egyptians to hold 51 percent of a company's capital and 40 percent of its directorships, this law implied a great loss in managerial authority for Anglo-Egyptian Oil and Socony-Vacuum if they intended to continue work in Egypt. While these two firms were willing to turn themselves into Egyptian joint stock companies and to take on a certain proportion of Egyptian directors, they refused to yield a majority of the shares to Egyptian investors.

The mining law was not the only source of discontent for the oil companies with the Egyptian state. During the war the government had regulated oil production and pricing to ensure cheap kerosene for the masses. The state had not dismantled the price regulations at the close of the war, largely because it feared social revolution and was determined to distribute essential commodities cheaply to the people. To enable the oil producers to sell kerosene cheaply the state established an oil stabilization fund which in theory guaranteed profits to the oil companies. The firms were to be allowed to charge remunerative prices for certain petroleum lines so that losses sustained in the sale of kerosene would be balanced out. In practice, however, the stabilization fund accumulated large deficits (as much as LE 1 million in 1949), and its operation was a constant source of friction between the state and the oil companies.[51] The government also made trouble over leases, blocked Anglo-Egyptian Oil's purchase of land at Suez needed to expand its refinery, and delayed the issuance of permits for foreign personnel seeking to enter the country.[52] These differences eventually showed up on the balance sheets; in 1951, for instance, Anglo-Egyptian Oil's profits fell from LE 720,001 to LE 207,310, and the reserve fund had to be used in order to pay the dividend (see table 4.2).

To make matters worse, in the early 1950s Anglo-Egyptian Oil was unwillingly involved against the Egyptian nationalists. Late in 1951 and early in 1952, just after the Wafdist government's abrogation of the Anglo-Egyptian Treaty of 1936 had set off guerrilla warfare against the British troops based in the Suez Canal area, the British military interdicted oil supplies from there to the Delta. The British soldiers cut off oil from the main pumping station on the Suez to Cairo pipeline, which was run by Anglo-Egyptian Oil and through which light oils flowed. They also interrupted the supply of heavy industrial oil which traveled by road and rail from the canal zone.[53] Although Anglo-Egyptian Oil vehemently opposed these measures, the Egyptian populace could not know this fact. Instead, the nationalists saw collusion between the military and this British firm. Not surprisingly, Anglo-Egyptian Oil received no relief in its squabbles with the Egyptian government during this period over the pricing of locally sold oil products. It claimed to have lost LE 2.7 million in 1953 and anticipated a further loss of LE 3.3 million in 1954 as a consequence of governmental financial controls.[54]

But the difficulties were almost entirely resolved by 1954. Both Anglo-Egyptian Oil and Socony-Vacuum were now confident of Egypt's economic future and were prepared to invest large sums of new money in exploration projects. The first step toward the resolution of tensions occurred when the oil companies agreed to become Egyptian joint stock companies so that they would be eligible for new exploration permits. Anglo-Egyptian Oil remained firmly opposed to allowing Egyptian majority participation in shareholding, but by becoming an Egyptian joint stock company, with a new and largely

Egyptian board, it won an exemption from the state on the shareholding issue.[55] Accordingly, in 1949 Anglo-Egyptian Oil moved the control and management of the firm to Egypt. It undertook to hold its board meetings in Cairo rather than in London. The board membership was completely altered. Other changes were carried out with a view to separating, in form at least, the parent firm from its affiliate. Anglo-Saxon Oil, which still owned 34 percent of the stock of Anglo-Egyptian Oil, renounced its formal management contract with Anglo-Egyptian Oil. That responsibility devolved upon N. V. de Bafaafsche Petroleum Mustschappij, which, while an affiliate of the Royal Dutch-Shell group, did not hold any of Anglo-Egyptian Oil's stock.[56] Shell Oil also distanced itself from its Egyptian affiliate. According to an internal Shell memorandum: "Authoritative advice could be given but any correspondence should be carried on by means of personal letters."[57]

Of course the changes were formal rather than substantial. Shell remained in control, exercising its influence now, however, mainly through its handpicked managing director and the chairman of the board of Anglo-Egyptian Oil. In a further effort to appease Egyptian official and public opinion, Anglo-Egyptian Oil improved its labor relations. It created a position for a labor adviser within the company. According to the British Chancery as well as expert Egyptian opinion, Anglo-Egyptian Oil turned itself into one of the best employers in the country.[58]

These alterations set the stage for the final oil accord, negotiated during 1954 and consummated only because of the personal intervention of Nasser himself.[59] The government brought pressure on Anglo-Egyptian Oil and Socony-Vacuum to compromise by offering oil prospecting licenses to a number of new firms—in effect breaking the oil exploration and production monopoly of these two companies. In 1954 the state negotiated new and large oil exploration concessions in Sinai and the Western and Eastern deserts with four oil conglomerates: Coronado, an American combine involving Continental Oil, Ohio Oil, and Amerada Petroleum; the Egyptian Oil Company; the General Oil Company of Hanover; and the National Oil Company of Egypt, a conglomerate of American, British, and Egyptian Companies.[60] But Anglo-Egyptian Oil and Socony-Vacuum also had leverage with the Egyptian government since they were the most experienced oil firms in Egypt and were prepared to spend as much as LE 6 million over a three-year period, provided that outstanding difficulties were resolved. Geoffrey Taitt, Anglo-Egyptian Oil's representative, warned that without an agreement on these questions he would be unable to persuade his board to increase the company's share capital or expand its operations in Egypt.[61]

An agreement was initialed in June 1954, but only "after a series of long and at times stormy meetings", which revealed to the Anglo-Egyptian Oil chief negotiator, Taitt, how divided the military rulers were and how deep-seated was the antipathy to foreign capital on the part of some of the officers. According to Taitt, General Salah Salem used negotiation sessions as a vehicle for excoriating Anglo-Egyptian Oil as an exploiter of the Egyptian people and as an arm of British colonial rule. According to the agreement the government of Egypt undertook to pay LE 2.5 million for oil supplies delivered by the Shell Company of Egypt. Anglo-Egyptian Oil and Socony-Vacuum would pay into the stabilization fund LE 2.7 million due to the government of Egypt as a consequence of the latter's right to purchase oil at a preferential rate. The Egyptian government would also pay Shell, acting for the other oil firms, LE 2.5 million due out of the stabilization fund, and would keep this fund in balance, if necessary by subsidizing the fund from general taxation to the extent of LE 2 million per year or by raising prices. In return, Anglo-Egyptian Oil and Socony-Vacuum signed leases to exploit the Ras Matarna concession and received licenses for sixty-one new prospecting areas. The two companies anticipated an expenditure of LE 4.5 million over a three-year period. Anglo-Egyptian Oil doubled its capital from LE 1.8 million to LE 3.6 million.[62]

The oil accord seemed to mark an important juncture in the development of the Egyptian political economy. The signals extended well beyond the oil companies themselves. They indicated the state's determination to work in harness with all forms of private capital, foreign as well as domestic.

Public utility concessionary companies—almost all of which were originally financed and run by foreigners—aroused great resentment against foreign capital in Egypt. These utility companies, like the oil firms, came into day-to-day contact with Egypt's urban population, for they supplied Egypt's major cities with electricity, water, gas, and transportation services. Although they tended to concentrate their services in the wealthier residential quarters, their trams, street lighting, and piped water were also part of the lifestyles of the less fortunate. Much of what was no doubt inevitable tension over rates and fees came to a head nonetheless during the 1930s when the urban populace complained bitterly against the companies' rates. If one looks, by way of example, at the newspaper *Shubra*, which carried information about this important, largely lower- and lower-middle-class Cairo suburb, one encounters a stream of complaints from the editors of the paper as well as its subscribers against all the public utility companies. The newspaper attacked the Cairo Water Company, the Cairo Tram Company, the Bus Company, and the Gas and Electric Company for exploiting the laboring poor, and accused these firms of being interested solely in accumulating large profits for their European shareholders.[63]

Elsewhere in urban Egypt the story was much the same. Newspaper articles regularly complained about the privileges enjoyed by these companies and detailed the one-sided concessions their original owners had negotiated with a weak Egyptian government. The press reproved the Alexandria municipality for having conceded (in 1879) a concession in perpetuity to the Alexandria Water Company.[64] Other agreements, it was observed, allowed companies to achieve large profits without placing restraints on the charges made against consumers.[65] As an example, the Cairo Electric Light and Power Supply Company, founded in 1906, allocated 5 percent of its profits up to LE 500 to its reserve and then divided the remainder of the profits 15 percent to the board and 85 percent to its shareholders. The government of Egypt and the municipality of Cairo did not share in profits, and provisions were not made to guarantee the reduction of rates if the profits were high.[66]

The campaign against the public utilities culminated in the passage of a stringent public utilities law in 1947, however, which asserted Egyptian state control over these firms. The edict stipulated that no new concession was to last more than thirty years. The profits of companies were limited to 10 percent of capital, plus a reserve fund not to exceed an additional 10 percent of capital. Profits beyond these levels had to be used to reduce charges and improve services and then had to be divided between the government and the company.[67]

The supreme European concessionaire and the most obvious symbol of European financial dominance in Egypt was the Suez Canal Company (Compagnie Universelle du Canal Maritime de Suez). The history of the original concession agreements negotiated by de Lesseps with Khedive Said, the sale of the Egyptian shares of the Canal Company in 1875 to British Prime Minister Benjamin Disraeli just as the company was beginning to turn a profit, and the substantial investment of Egyptian labor and money in the company for little or no return was a story on the lips of every Egyptian nationalist. Even Egyptian moderates in the nineteenth century believed that the Canal Company had ruthlessly exploited Egypt and that the presence of the canal had brought about the British occupation of the country. Before World War I Tal'at Harb had written a ringing denunciation of the Suez Canal Company (*Qana al-Suwis*, published in Cairo in 1910) showing how much Egypt had contributed to its success and how little good it had brought the country. Harb's book, in fact, was written in opposition to a British effort to have the canal concession extended from 1968 to 2008 in return for turning over a proportion of the profits to the Egyptian government. Although these payments would have brought Egypt a financial return on this increasingly valuable asset, the Egyptian parliament rejected the proposal on patriotic grounds.

Complaints against the Canal Company continued during the interwar years and reached a crescendo after World War II, when calls for its nationalization were heard from every quarter. Undoubtedly the most vigorous of the nationalist critics was Mustafa al-Hifnawi, who in his public speeches, newspaper articles, and pamphlets and books attributed Egypt's backwardness to the baleful influence of the canal and its company.[68] Hifnawi alternated calls for the immediate nationalization of the company with pleas that Egypt prepare itself for 1968 when the original concession would terminate and the canal would officially become Egyptian property. Hifnawi's attacks were a cause of alarm to the Canal Company since his close ties with Egypt's majority party, the Wafd, which was reported to have financed his education in Paris, suggested that his stance reflected party thinking.[69]

The widespread antagonism against the Canal Company stemmed not only from the much maligned original concession but also from Egypt's inability to make the company more responsive to the country's political and economic needs. The battles on these points spilled over from the negotiating rooms and inflamed nationalist sentiment. The Egyptian press complained that the Suez Canal Company was a state unto itself and that it used its international prestige to resist legitimate Egyptian demands to trim its vast political powers and to share in its financial bounty.

The first clash occurred in the 1930s and led to an accord in 1937, by which Egyptian representation on the board of the company was mandated (two members). The Egyptian work force was increased, and the company undertook to contribute at least LE 300,00 to the state per year.[70] These negotiations were a prelude to more intense ones carried out in 1948 and 1949. Prodded by the nationalist press, the government sought to apply the 1947 joint stock company law to the Canal Company. In spite of its international status and mixed board of directors the Suez Canal Company was legally an Egyptian joint stock company. The rigorous application of the 1947 company law would have meant that 40 percent of the thirty-two directors would have to be Egyptians, and a high proportion of the clerical and regular work force as well. During the dispute the government threatened to take the company to the Egyptian courts.[71] Finally, a compromise was reached on March 7, 1949, which greatly increased the Egyptian presence in the company, but did not require the company to conform fully to the 1947 law.

This important agreement stipulated that Egyptians were to fill the next five vacancies on the board, increasing the total of Egyptian directors to seven. The Egyptianization of personnel was to go forward in a vigorous way, with the goal of bringing the company into compliance with the 1947 law, but the company would not have to accomplish its Egyptianization program in the same three-year period allotted to other joint stock companies. Egyptian pilots were to be hired wherever possible. Finally the company agreed to pay a 7 percent tax on its gross profits, bringing the amount collected from £200,000 to an estimated £800,000, with £350,000 guaranteed as a minimum payment.[72]

This comprehensive agreement notwithstanding, quarrels continued apace in the 1950s. Repeated disputes occurred over the selection of the new Egyptian directors. The government, in particular the king, wanted to select the Egyptian representatives, while the company often opposed these nominees—particularly Ahmad 'Abbud, whom the company feared because of his nationalism, egoism, and presumed sympathy with British goals. The company was fearful that an individual of 'Abbud's stature would have to be put on the all-powerful Comité de Direction and would politicize the discussions of this executive body.[73]

The chief bones of contention between the Canal Company and knowledgeable Egyptian critics were the growing profits and massive financial surpluses which began to appear in the decade after World War II. The issue of their use—whether to reduce canal dues, to increase dividends, or to invest in Egypt and abroad—became a matter of intense discussion, not in this instance so much in the press (where the issue was perhaps too complex) but in high-level political and financial circles. There can be little question that the earnings of the Canal Company were a temptation to the financially hard-pressed yet economically ambitious Egyptian government well before Nasser nationalized the Suez Canal Company in 1956.

Canal finances had been transformed by the increase of traffic, particularly oil tanker traffic, after 1945. Net profits, which had hovered around Fr 3,000 million to Fr 4,000 million between the wars rose more than threefold in 1948 and remained at this new plateau, even increasing a little, between 1948 and 1955. Dividends did not rise nearly so sharply, increasing by about one and a half times between 1946 and 1955, (see graph 4.1). The company was awash in funds after the war. The statutory reserve increased from Fr 305 million to Fr 430 million in 1948 and remained at that figure until the nationalization crisis. Other funds—the contingency fund, the extraordinary reserve, the amortization reserve, and the pension fund—rose sharply (see table 4.3).

Just what was to be done with these funds totaling Fr 38,775,279,231 or £39.6 million in 1955 was a question of the greatest financial and economic importance to the Canal Company and the Egyptian government. D. R. Serpell of the British Treasury, responsible for the British interests in the Suez Canal Company, counseled a sharp reduction in canal dues and a diminution of receipts and reserves.[74] He justified his position on the grounds of affording less temptation to the Egyptians to nationalize the company. No doubt as a representative of the leading shipping nation, he had other reasons for espousing this position. His stance found little support among the company directors, whose arguments in favor of retaining the existing rating structure were compelling. In the first place the company had an obligation to increase its capital reserves and secure its pension funds in light of the expiration of the concession in 1968. And secondly, the firm also realized that any effort to reduce tolls and thus diminish receipts, dividends, and reserves was likely to be viewed with intense suspicion in Egyptian quarters. Egypt received 7 percent of the gross profits and had nothing to gain from reduced shipping charges.[75]

Although the company's position on this issue was unassailable, its use of its growing financial resources was easy to reproach. In 1951 the company created an investment trust and transferred funds from its well-stocked financial reserves to this body for investment overseas.[76] Within a year of the creation of the investment trust the Canal Company had moved Fr 9,626 million (book value; market value Fr 12,000 million) into foreign securities.[77] At the same time it had rejected an Egyptian proposal to grant LE 1 million in support of a projected steel plant at Helwan.[78] One of the British delegates sitting on the board of the Suez Canal Company called the investment trust nothing less than an international financial holding company, a fact made palpable when Jacques Georges-Picot was named Egyptian director-general of the company—Georges-Picot was not a canal man, but an investment expert; he already sat on numerous French companies and was widely admired because of his knowledge of European and North American money markets.[79]

Just how much the Suez Canal Company had evolved from an Egyptian joint stock canal company to a multinational financial holding company can be seen from the final settlement arranged between the company and the Egyptian government following nationalization. Although some of the estimates can be questioned, they reveal the magnitude of overseas involvement. During the negotiations Charles-Roux, president of the company, claimed that the company's assets outside Egypt totaled £41 million and those in Egypt £70 million even though in an earlier annual report all assets had been valued at £83 million, of which the movable and fixed assets in Egypt were said to be worth £22.4 million.[80] In the final compensation accord of 1958 the Egyptian government agreed to pay the company £29 million for its Egyptian properties and to leave to the shareholders all the company's assets outside Egypt.[81] The Compagnie Financière de Suez was then created to take over the overseas investment activities of the now defunct Suez Canal Company.[82]

By its slowness in Egyptianizing and by its accumulation of large profits, the Suez Canal Company both angered and tempted the Egyptian government; yet the Canal Company, albeit reluctantly and gradually, had been setting its house in order in the 1950s. It was becoming a real boon to Egypt's economic development. The number of Egyptian directors was on the increase. The proportions of Egyptian clerical and working personnel were rising, and the company had begun to finance the training of Egyptian pilots. Perhaps most importantly of all, the government persuaded the company in June 1956 to set aside LE 21 million from its reserves to finance large-scale development projects in Egypt. LE 10 million were ready for subscription in 1956.[83] Thus, even in the case of the Suez Canal Company a number of burning fiscal and political issues had been resolved by 1956. The company had clearly indicated that it was prepared to make changes in response to nationalist demands.[84]

Some Conclusions

The effort to understand the expropriation of Bradford and Calico investments in Egypt—when they seemed to be an unalloyed advantage to the country and a weight and worry to the parent companies—has involved a long trek through the histories of other important business firms in Egypt. The examination of foreign capital from the vantage point of individual firms has demonstrated that the Bradford and Calico stories are far from unusual. Egyptian shareholding and managerial control were on the rise. Egyptian legislation was forcing less easily dominated firms to pay heed to the interests and needs of the Egyptian economy.

By 1955–56, then, just prior to the withdrawal of Western support for the Aswan dam, which precipitated the nationalization of the Suez Canal Company, many of the outstanding issues involving foreign capital had been resolved in ways acceptable to foreign companies and attractive and beneficial to the Egyptian government. The harsh mining law of 1948 had been softened. Negotiations with Anglo-Egyptian Oil and Socony-Vacuum had ended the war of words between these firms and the state. The new military government headed by Nasser had altered the much-criticized company law of 1947, granting exemptions from taxation on commercial and industrial profits for approved schemes and reducing the percentage of capital to be owned by Egyptians from 51 to 49 percent.[85] Although the Nasser regime had also sequestered some joint stock companies with which it had ongoing disputes (the Sugar Company was eventually liquidated in 1955), most of the signals coming from the military, even in the middle of 1956, indicated support for foreign capital.

The nationalization of British, French, and Jewish capital in 1957 and Belgian capital in 1960 and 1961 marked a watershed in Egyptian economic history. These steps led to the massive emigration of the foreign communities resident in Egypt. It is hard to avoid the conclusion that the actions arose less from economic motives than from political and social factors. Lacking records of the discussions of the military councils (and as the memoirs of the military leaders are curiously silent on this question), we draw our conclusions indirectly and circumstantially. To be sure, the economic factors cannot be ignored. The nationalization of the Suez Canal Company had a large economic and fiscal component. The profits and foreign exchange earning capacity of the company were deemed essential for Egypt's economic development. Yet without question the canal constituted Egypt's emotive symbol of colonial subjugation. All Egyptian nationalists of whatever persuasion ached to take over the canal. No possibility existed of an extension of the canal concession. Nor could Egyptian politicians be persuaded to allow an international body to operate the canal. The only question was exactly when Egypt would assert its sovereignty over this waterway, and the withdrawal of Western aid for the Aswan dam served as the perfect pretext.

Yet events themselves shaped the evolution of the Egyptian economy. The new military leaders, despite their earlier and vague assertions in favor of social justice and against foreign and monopoly capital, had made peace with foreign capital and believed that foreign investment could serve Egyptian development purposes. A decision to withdraw aid for the Aswan Dam project unleashed a chain of events, including the nationalization of the Suez Canal Company, which led to a British-French-Israeli attempted reconquest of the country. The uneasy understanding reached between the military leaders and foreign capital was breached. Those in the government who favored expunging foreign economic influences were given their chance.

It is difficult to resist the conclusion that social and political factors loomed larger than economics in the dispossessing of foreign capitalists. The mentality of the military leaders was formed in the radical environment of the 1930s. Their ideas on political economy were crystallized during the depression when nationalist politicians squabbled with foreign capitalists over foreign capitulatory privilege (finally abolished in 1937), over shouldering a fairer share of Egypt's tax burden, and making a more determined effort to provide employment and training for educated Egyptians. The men of Nasser's and Sadat's generation imbibed the radical antiforeign and in some cases anticapitalist rhetoric of Young Egypt and the Muslim Brotherhood in an era when foreign capital did unquestionably hold a privileged and arrogant position in the Egyptian economy and when foreigners were contemptuous of Egyptian ways. When indeed in 1956 and 1957 foreign banks and insurance companies aligned themselves with Egypt's enemies, even balking at financing the cotton crop of that year and favoring foreigners over native Egyptian clients in loans and insurance arrangements, these images of an aloof and unresponsive foreign capital reasserted themselves. Certainly, wealthy foreigners lived socially aloof lives, comfortably ensconced in their exclusive residential quarters in Cairo and Alexandria. They were largely unsympathetic on many nationalist issues. But foreign capital no longer enjoyed the autonomy it had possessed in an earlier era. A succession of Egyptian governments had enacted legislation which ensured that the successes enjoyed by foreign businessmen would also benefit the Egyptian people.

The Egyptianization of foreign capital was the culmination of a long and bitter campaign against the overweening and privileged presence of foreign capital in Egypt. The irony of the story is that just at a time when foreign corporations were coming under Egyptian control and were being bent to Egyptian purposes the state was driven by anger to liquidate this foreign business presence.

Tables

Table 2.1
Egypt's Foreign Trade and Trade with United Kingdom, 1909-1952

	Total Imports LE	Imports from United Kingdom LE	Percentage	Total Exports LE	Exports to United Kingdom LE	Percentage
1909	22,230,499	6,743,678	30	26,076,239	13,099,910	50
1910	23,552,826	7,311,218	31	28,944,461	14,343,381	50
1911	27,227,118	8,557,296	31	28,598,991	13,958,058	49
1912	25,908,000	7,991,000	31	34,574,000	16,022,000	46
1913	27,865,000	8,496,000	30	31,662,000	13,648,000	43
1919	47,409,717	21,840,957	46	75,888,321	40,222,821	53
1920	101,880,963	37,894,760	37	85,467,061	36,343,184	43
1921	55,507,984	16,937,815	31	36,356,062	17,045,830	47
1922	43,333,938	14,731,622	34	48,716,418	23,035,915	47
1923	45,276,963	14,771,677	33	58,387,327	28,354,293	49
1924	50,736,918	13,993,584	28	65,733,935	31,955,625	49
1925	58,224,895	14,660,664	25	59,198,662	26,167,972	44
1926	52,400,059	11,405,307	22	41,759,391	18,921,153	45
1927	48,685,785	12,482,606	26	48,340,503	19,138,089	40
1928	52,043,969	11,326,242	22	56,165,258	21,532,193	38
1929	56,089,512	11,895,512	21	51,751,984	17,958,982	35
1930	47,488,328			31,941,592		
1931	31,528,167	7,134,416	23	27,937,113	10,026,508	36
1932	27,425,691	6,586,724	24	26,987,417	10,373,014	38
1933	26,766,991	6,189,520	23	28,842,436	12,004,919	42
1934	29,303,723	6,486,611	22	31,055,759	9,947,871	32
1935	32,238,859	7,360,310	23	35,693,162	12,636,669	35
1936	31,515,555	7,526,926	24	32,978,400	12,491,478	38
1937	38,038,098	8,288,018	22	39,759,066	12,446,625	31
1938	36,934,373	8,496,512	23	29,342,486	9,863,701	34
1939	34,090,716	9,430,273	28	34,080,913	12,322,690	36
1945	60,475,769	10,955,431	18	41,629,998	11,408,030	27
1946	81,094,217	24,954,363	31	63,680,509	21,221,722	33
1947	100,246,974	21,601,771	22	85,716,069	23,781,700	28
1948	161,218,448	36,293,773	23	140,740,670	41,248,174	29
1949	167,519,216	37,984,924	23	135,671,053	23,594,048	17
1950	204,681,999	41,323,182	20	172,958,680	37,090,252	22
1951	235,840,586	41,926,742	18	200,639,051	38,571,673	19
1952	220,690,944	29,649,090	13	142,851,388	6,399,625	4

Source: Egypt, Ministry of Finance, Statistical Department, *Annuaire Statistique.*

Table 2.2
British Trade with Egypt, 1913–1952

	British Exports to Egypt £	Percentage of Total British Exports	British Imports from Egypt £	Percentage of Total British Imports
1913	9,805,639	1.9	16,134,777	2.1
1919	19,405,263	2.4	53,972,906	3.3
1920	43,643,665	3.3	48,682,688	2.5
1921	18,884,073	2.7	23,457,908	2.2
1922	15,366,886	2.2	27,926,583	2.8
1923	15,073,468	2.0	29,747,472	2.7
1924	15,117,525	1.9	34,231,751	2.7
1925	16,424,231	2.1	28,094,217	2.1
1926	11,030,330	1.7	20,414,446	1.6
1927	12,564,387	1.8	20,823,833	1.7
1928	11,185,647	1.5	24,144,368	2.0
1929	12,576,232	1.7	21,540,261	1.8
1930	9,807,690	1.7	12,392,242	1.2
1931	6,650,427	1.7	10,202,114	1.2
1932	6,509,981	1.8	9,490,260	1.4
1933	6,260,049	1.7	11,550,939	1.7
1934	6,528,322	1.6	10,483,542	1.4
1935	7,631,373	1.8	11,677,567	1.5
1936	7,756,411	1.8	12,691,647	1.5
1937	7,878,890	1.5	13,374,165	1.3
1938	8,689,015	1.8	11,103,933	1.2
1939	9,670,053	2.2	11,522,322	1.3
1940	8,968,468	2.2	13,190,020	1.1
1941	9,018,048	2.5	8,970,198	.8
1942	8,901,901	2.3	15,643,591	1.3
1943	4,509,341	1.3	11,002,211	.6
1944	5,919,235	1.8	13,143,825	.6
1945	11,251,147	2.6	13,152,206	.9
1946	23,388,391	2.6	14,620,406	1.1
1947	21,969,636	1.9	13,240,351	.7
1948	34,101,055	2.2	47,545,666	2.3
1949	35,980,906	2.0	28,915,472	1.3
1950	42,442,154	2.0	39,396,556	1.5
1951	40,586,453	1.6	47,320,926	1.2
1952	32,540,704	1.3	12,774,490	.5

Source: United Kingdom, Customs and Excise Department, *Trade with Foreign Countries and British Possessions,* 1913–1952.

Table 2.3
Main British Exports to Egypt, 1909-1939

	Coal		Textiles		Machinery and Metals	
	Value LE	Percentage of Total Egyptian Coal Imports	Value LE	Percentage of Total Egyptian Textile Imports	Value LE	Percentage of Total Egyptian Machinery and Metals Imports
1909	1,177,544	44	3,751,733	64	936,393	48
1910	1,233,472	44	4,068,115	61	1,138,709	48
1911	1,327,462	45	4,848,999	59	1,415,444	48
1912	1,483,314	48	4,196,002	61	1,311,111	45
1913	1,874,368	49	4,108,360	60	1,488,054	47
1919	2,665,497	68	13,207,183	70	2,553,100	68
1920	2,692,409	22	22,771,387	66	6,656,690	56
1921	1,359,070	22	9,291,385	63	3,309,760	45
1922	1,381,177	36	8,980,549	60	1,927,257	36
1923	1,663,265	42	8,776,996	53	1,944,498	36
1924	1,751,615	42	7,713,955	45	2,296,794	34
1925	1,841,180	38	7,544,024	42	2,935,316	35
1926	913,991	21	4,847,087	36	3,378,679	39
1927	1,915,544	45	5,130,549	37	3,253,392	39
1928	1,510,082	40	4,710,625	31	2,912,455	32
1929	1,702,581	39	4,715,250	29	3,003,431	31
1930						
1931	1,334,154	46	2,080,443	27	1,673,193	35
1932	1,171,438	37	2,240,879	29	1,320,930	35
1933	1,067,229	36	2,077,189	26	1,164,939	32
1934	1,147,446	37	1,922,659	23	1,404,454	32
1935	1,495,441	39	1,764,738	22	1,770,915	35
1936	981,438	32	2,369,491	31	1,752,651	34
1937	1,521,736	33	2,220,632	25	1,842,808	28
1938	1,672,111	36	1,693,602	24	1,919,432	29
1939	1,983,563	41	1,531,542	27	2,098,217	33

Source: Egypt, Ministry of Finance, Statistical Department, *Annuaire Statistique.*

Table 2.4
Capitalization and Profitability of British Textile Firms

	Bleachers Association		Bradford Dyers		Calico Printers	
	Capital Employed £ 000	Profit as % of Employed Capital	Capital Employed £ 000	Profit as % of Employed Capital	Capital Employed £ 000	Profit as % of Employed Capital
1910–11	7,335	5.6	5,695	5.5	8,201	6.1
1911–12	7,519	6.3	5,758	5.8	8,344	5.0
1912–13	7,635	7.0	5,820	5.5	8,279	6.1
1913–14	7,821	6.7	5,888	5.7	8,427	2.7
1920–21	8,870	6.9	6,878	9.0	9,218	4.1
1921–22	8,986	8.4	6,881	4.6	9,218	4.1
1922–23	9,133	9.7	6,881	14.5	9,118	10.2
1923–24	9,260	9.7	7,064	11.3	9,417	7.1
1924–25	9,395	10.1	7,206	9.9	9,555	8.7
1925–26	9,562	9.1	7,399	6.0	9,703	3.5
1926–27	9,549	4.5	7,290	4.5	9,618	3.7

Source: United Kingdom, Committee on Industry and Trade, *Survey of Textile Industries,* 1928, p.42.

Table 2.5
Calico Major Merchandising Agents—Cairo

Major Mercantile Firms of Cairo	Principal Travelers	Number of Years as Agents	Location
David Ades and Son	Raffoul Cohen	7	Lower Egypt
	Khalifa Soued	20	Lower Egypt
	Siahou Pinto	5	Upper Egypt
Nessim Ades and Son	Zaki Harari	10	Upper Egypt
	Moussa Douekzo	20	Lower Egypt
B. Nathan Successors	Jacques Benjamine	13	Lower Egypt
	Abdel Rahman el-Habbog	1	Upper Egypt
Nessim Haim Bigio	Muhammad el-Negami	20	Lower Egypt
	Labib Gaafer	20	Lower Egypt
	Haroun Frangi	15	Upper Egypt
Habilo Toledano and Sons	David Ades	2	Upper Egypt
	M. Ezra Marcus	10	Lower Egypt
Em Casdagli and Sons	Ahmad Mahmud	10	Lower Egypt
	M. Antoun	10	Lower Egypt
Gubbay Freres	Selim Rekib	10	Upper Egypt
B. and A. Levy	Abdel Latif Bayoumi	20	Cairo–Minya
	Moussa Sabah	5	Minya–Aswan
	Kamel Effendi	5	Lower Egypt

Source: McCulloch to Railton, December 24, 1935, CPA Secretariat Group M75, File 102, Manchester General Library.

Table 2.6
Production of Egyptian Weaving and Rate of Increase

	Production m²	Rate of Increase %	Imports of Cotton Piece Goods m²
1930	14,000,000		
1931	20,000,000	42	147,004,859
1932	24,500,000	22	174,489,951
1933	29,000,000	18	196,835,640
1934	38,000,000	31	182,056,841
1935	34,500,000	-9.2	193,403,415
1936	55,000,000	59	169,629,259
1937	66,500,000	21	169,522,178
1938	110,000,000	66	137,428,872
1939	159,500,000	45	82,474,308
1940	185,000,000	16	66,052,446
1941	200,000,000	8	66,696,073

Source: Eman, *L'Industrie du Coton en Égypte*, pp. 33 and 34.

Table 3.1
Consumption of Locally Produced and Imported Cotton Goods in 000,000 kgs

	1938	1948
Local Production of Yarn	20.5	49.7
Imported Yarn	.8	.3
Less: Exported Yarn	.4	—
Net Yarn Supply	20.9	50.0
Local Production of Cotton Goods	20.3	48.7
Imported Cotton Goods	17.6	4.8
Total Available Supply	37.9	53.5

Source: National Bank of Egypt, *Economic Bulletin,* vol. 4, no. 2, 1951, pp. 95–103.

Table 3.2
Cotton Production 1939-1956

	Total Production		Misr Spinning and Weaving Co.		Misr Fine Spinning and Weaving Co.		Two Factories' Proportion of Total	
	Yarn metric tons	Cotton Piece Goods 000,000m²	Yarn metric tons	Cotton Piece Goods 000,000m²	Yarn metric tons	Cotton Piece Goods 000,000m²	Yarn %	Cotton Piece Goods %
1939			15.2	76.9				
1940			13.6	66.7				
1941					2.8	16.7		
1942			14.7	67.8	4.3	22.3		
1943			16.4	66.5	4.0	27.4		
1944			16.9	70.7	3.9	28.0		
1945			16.5	76.1	4.6	30.5		
1946			18.9	83.8	4.9	32.1		
1947			17.6	80.1	5.2	37.1		
1948			19.8	92.5	6.5	50.0		
1949	54.3		18.0	88.6	7.7	50.1	47.3	
1950	49.0		15.0	78.6	8.9	50.5	48.8	
1951	52.8	210.0	16.0	84.9	9.0	60.1	47.3	69.0
1952	55.7	219.8	16.7	92.2	9.1	61.7	46.3	70.0
1953	59.3	233.4	17.8	85.8	8.2	58.9	43.8	62.0
1954	64.3	240.9	19.7	95.2	8.7	62.6	44.2	65.5
1955	73.1	245.7	21.2	99.3	8.3	62.7	40.4	65.9
1956	75.0	258.1	22.7	99.8	8.1	61.4	41.4	62.5

Sources: various issues of National Bank of Egypt, *Economic Bulletins* and *Stock Exchange Yearbook of Egypt.*

Table 3.3
Capitalization of Egyptian Textile Companies Before and After World War II (LE)

	1939	1946
Industries Fibres Textiles (1937)	44,000	200,000
Société Égyptienne de Tissage et Tricotage (1934)	50,000	200,000
Usines Textiles al-Kahira (1936)	60,000	95,000
Clothing and Equipment Company (1920)ʾ	51,000	200,000
Établissements Industriels Pour la Soie et le Coton (1940)		500,000
Fabrique Égyptienne des Textiles, "Ka-Bo" (1935)	40,000	100,000
Manufacture Égyptienne de Bonneterie et Tricotage, el-Nil (1939)	8,000	12,000
Manufacture de Textiles Égyptiens, "Matexa" (1941)		150,000
Nile Textile Company (1941)		400,000
Orient Linen Company (1941)		250,000
Société Égyptienne de Filature et Tissage de Laine (1937)	40,000	500,000
Société Égyptienne de l'Industrie de Bonneterie, "La Bonneterie" (1935)	100,000	100,000
Société Industrielle des Fils et Textiles, "Spahi" (1941)		500,000
	393,000	3,207,000

Sources: The *Stock Exchange Yearbook of Egypt* and individual articles in *Revue d'Égypte économique et financière.*

Table 3.4
Major Textile Firms: Capitalization and Profitability, 1939 and 1946

	Capital LE		Reserves LE		Net Profit LE		Dividend PT	
	1939	1946	1939	1946	1939	1946	1939	1946
Filature	487,500	780,000	213,147	416,764	134,821	350,384	55	140
Misr Spinning & Weaving	1,000,000	1,000,000	105,593	2,272,031	52,679	458,578	28	150
Misr Fine Spinning & Weaving (1941)	500,000	500,000		1,110,716	48,028	310,553	32	140
Beida Dyers	400,000	400,000	7,342	1,628,704	7,342	145,457	20	140
SEIT	500,000	500,000	(23,282)[a]		(48,783)	(267,893)	(30)	
Total	2,887,500	3,180,000	326,082	5,428,215	242,870[b]	1,264,972[c]		
Average Dividend							33.75[d]	142.5[e]

[a] I have bracketed the data on SEIT because I was unable to obtain a full time series. Thus, in calculating overall totals for reserves and net profits and estimating percentages of profitability and average dividends, I have left SEIT out of my calculations but included individual figures where I found them.

[b] 7.6% of nominal capital and reserves

[c] 15.6% of nominal capital and reserves

[d] 8.4% of the nominal value of a share (LE 4)

[e] 35.6% of the nominal value of a share (LE 4)

Table 3.5
Profit Rates of Major Textile Firms as Percentage of Nominal Capital and Reserves, 1939-1945

	Filature	Misr Spinning & Weaving	Misr Fine Spinning & Weaving	Beida Dyers
1939		4.8		
1939-40				6.5
1941 (9mths)		10.9		
1941-42	28.5	15.6	16.7	29.0
1942-43	38.7			23.2
1943-44	27.7		20.5	17.0
1944-45	27.1	13.5	24.1	11.2
1945-46	29.3	14.0	19.3	7.2

Table 3.6
Profit Rates of Major Textile Firms as Percentage of Nominal Capital Only, 1939-1945

	1939-40	1940-41	1941-42	1942-43	1943-44	1944-45	1945-46
Filature	47.4	41.1	35.9	53.0	40.1	41.0	44.9
Misr Spinning and Weaving Company	5.3	14.5	23.8	32.3	34.4	39.3	45.9
Misr Fine Spinning and Weaving Company		9.6	22.0	38.2	40.0	51.6	62.1
Beida Dyers	6.7	19.1	35.0	40.6	44.3	32.2	36.4
SEIT	19.8	25.5	33.7	76.2	46.1	52.9	53.6

Table 3.7

Profit Rates of Other Textile Firms as Percentage of Nominal Capital, 1939–1946

	1941	1942	1944	1945	1946
Établissements Industriels Pour la Soie et le Coton (1940)	23.0	30.0	21.6	8.2	
Industrie Fibres Textiles (1937)		45.2	34.2	17.7	
Misr Silk Weaving Company (1927)		50.8	12.8	31.1	
Société Égyptienne de Tissage et Tricotage (1934)			11.4	11.7	
Usines Textiles al-Kahira (1936)		9.4			7.4

	1941–42	1942–43	1943–44	1944–45	1945–46	1946–47
Fabrique Égyptienne des Textiles, "Ka-Bo" (1933)	30.4	26.4	35.2	18.1		27.9
Société Égyptienne de Filature et Tissage de Laine (1937)	32.2		36.0	22.3		
Société Égyptienne de l'Industrie de Bonneterie, "La Bonneterie" (1935)						

Table 3.8
Net Profits Compared with Capital and Reserves of the Eight Firms
in Table 3.7 (1945)

	Capital & Reserves LE	Net Profits LE
Établissements Industriels Pour la Soie et le Coton (1940)	512,618	42,181
Industrie Fibres Textiles (1937)	170,963	30,237
Misr Silk Weaving Company (1927)	625,371	194,266
Société Égyptienne de Tissage et Tricotage (1934)	297,575	34,725
Usines Textiles al-Kahira (1936)	163,947[a]	12,091
Fabrique Égyptienne des Textiles, "Ka-Bo" (1933)	214,436[a]	59,756
Société Égyptienne de Filature et Tissage de Laine (1937)	544,380	98,601
Société Égyptienne de l'Industrie de Bonneterie, "La Bonneterie" (1935)	155,355	34,718
Total	2,684,645	496,575[b]

[a] 1946 fiscal year.
[b] Or 18.5% of nominal capital and reserves.

Table 3.9
Financial Data on the Major Textile Firms

	1946–47	1950–51	1955–56
	Nominal Capitalization, LE		
Filature	780,000	780,000	780,000
Misr Spinning & Weaving	1,000,000	2,000,000	2,000,000
Misr Fine Spinning & Weaving	500,000	1,000,000	1,000,000
Beida Dyers	500,000	1,000,000	1,000,000
SEIT	500,000	500,000	500,000
Total	3,280,000	5,280,000	5,280,000
	Reserves, LE		
Filature	434,283	429,794	480,000
Misr Spinning & Weaving	2,517,888	3,501,397	8,242,295
Misr Fine Spinning & Weaving	1,706,913	1,012,136	7,367,115
Beida Dyers	2,406,681	1,427,315	2,814,168
Total	7,065,765	6,370,642	18,903,578
	Net Profit, LE (as %age of Capital & Reserves)		
Filature	350,384 (28.9)	337,296 (27.9)	297,227 (23.6)
Misr Spinning & Weaving	459,777 (13.1)	595,314 (10.8)	786,044 (7.7)
Misr Fine Spinning & Weaving	311,891 (14.1)	392,642 (19.5)	509,987 (6.1)
Beida Dyers	178,296 (6.1)	250,630 (10.3)	630,730 (19.0)
Total	1,300,348 (12.6)	1,575,882 (13.5)	2,223,988 (9.2)
	Dividend, PT (as %age of Nominal Value of Share)		
Filature	140 (35)	130 (32.5)	90 (22.5)
Misr Spinning & Weaving	150 (37.5)	100 (25)	135 (33.75)
Misr Fine Spinning & Weaving	150 (37.5)	100 (25)	135 (33.75)
Beida Dyers	150 (37.5)	100 (25)	135 (33.75)

Table 3.10
Profits of Major Textile Firms as Percentage of Nominal Capital

	Filature	Misr Spinning & Weaving	Misr Fine Spinning & Weaving	Beida Dyers	SEIT
1945-46	44.9	45.9	62.1	36.4	53.6
1946-47	44.9	46.0	62.4	35.7	51.3
1947-48	45.2	45.8	63.3	37.6	55.8
1948-49	44.3	45.7	63.0	37.9	3.1
1949-50	41.2	46.1	62.1	42.0	28.2
1950-51	42.3	29.8	39.3	25.1	29.2
1951-52	32.7	30.3	38.5	25.1	-7.9
1952-53	33.0	30.3	39.0	25.1	19.0
1953-54	25.6	30.2	38.8	60.1	23.7
1954-55	43.1	44.0	46.5	73.2	
1955-56	38.1	39.3	31.0	63.1	
Average	40.5	39.4	51.5	41.9	28.4

Table 3.11
Net Profits as Percentage of Nominal Capital among Textile Firms Listed in the Stock Exchange Yearbook of Egypt and Having a Nominal Capital of LE 95,000 or More

	1945–46	1946–47
Industries Fibres Textiles	18.5	11.7
Société Égyptienne de Tissage et Tricotage	17.4	18.5
Misr Silk Weaving Company	59.3	44.3
Usines Textiles al-Kahira	12.7	5.6
Alexandria Spinning and Weaving Company		
Clothing and Equipment Company	15.8	7.1
Cotton Spinning, Weaving and Dyeing Company, "Karnak"	19.6	15.4
al-Tawil Spinning and Weaving Company		
Etablissements Industriels Pour la Soie et le Coton	19.2	19.4
Fabrique Égyptienne des Textiles, "Ka-Bo"	60.2	29.9
Fayoum Textile Company		2.5
Manufacture de Textiles Égyptiens, Matexa	-2.2	13.0
Nile Textile Company	18.6	20.9
Orient Linen Industry	4.4	6.3
Selected Textile Industries Association		12.8
Société al-Chark Pour la Filature et le Tissage		9.6
Société Arabe de Filature et de Tissage		
Société Égyptienne de Filature et Tissage de Laine	20.9	23.8
Société Égyptienne de l'Industrie de Bonneterie, "La Bonneterie"	27.8	-38.0
Société Égyptienne "Nouzha" de Filature et Tissage		1.2
Société Misr Pour la Rayonne		
Société Nationale de Textile, "Memphis"		
Société des Usines el-Shourbaghi Pour la Filature, le Tissage, et le Tricot		
United Spinning and Weaving Company		

1947–48	1948–49	1949–50	1950–51	1951–52	1952–53	1953–54	1954–55	1955–56	Avg.
0.7	-0.9	12.9	7.2	-1.9	0.8	-2.4	-9.2	-5.9	3.4
8.5	6.9	8.3	6.6	-11.5	8.7	2.5	5.6	5.6	7.0
31.3	-5.2	-7.6	16.0	11.5	15.4	14.2	18.3	13.3	18.0
5.5	6.0	10.2	5.7	10.7	2.6	2.3	9.4		7.1
1.2	15.8	27.9	30.4	0.7	9.0	13.8	14.0	0.01	12.5
6.1	0.06	6.3							7.1
15.3	0.09	-6.3	8.2	0.7	3.9	6.7	3.2		6.7
		18.9	26.3	15.2	14.1	26.3	33.5	25.5	21.4
22.9	11.4	46.5	27.0						24.4
24.1	20.0	20.1	23.1	20.0	20.0	19.4	22.3	23.3	25.7
9.4	5.3	8.6	5.6	-7.8	7.8	4.5	4.4	4.4	4.5
8.1	6.0	10.0	13.0	9.3	18.7	26.5	26.5	26.8	14.2
21.0	17.3	26.8	27.7	-3.7	-5.2	0.4	9.3	6.1	12.7
0.01	-13.1	-3.2	-14.8	-43.9	0.0	-0.4	1.2	5.9	-5.2
13.0	11.6	15.3	16.2	15.2	17.2	9.6	15.0	17.9	14.4
15.2	18.6	36.3	14.1	-5.0	6.8	10.2	5.0	8.9	12.0
	5.8	12.3	24.4	-14.4	9.7	20.3	27.7	28.5	14.3
26.7	17.6	17.6	4.5	7.0	17.0	17.1	18.7	18.6	17.2
			9.2	-2.9	0.1	-18.8	6.9	4.9	-1.4
1.0			28.9	-18.1	5.5	12.2	14.5	8.4	6.7
0.0	0.2	5.7	14.8	14.8	14.9	18.0	20.8	20.5	12.2
		7.6	7.2	-1.4	-4.3	10.4	-8.2	-5.9	-2.2
7.8	-1.7	14.5	13.7	4.6	-4.2	3.9	12.3	21.2	8.0
		6.9	6.9	3.2	8.5	12.3	28.3	17.6	12.0

Table 3.12
Net Profit of Textile Firms
as Percentage of Nominal Capital and Reserves

	1945–46		1955–56	
	Nominal Capital and Reserves LE	Net Profit %	Nominal Capital and Reserves LE	Net Profit %
Industries Fibres Textiles	257,109	14.4	130,000	–5.9
Société Égyptienne de Tissage et Tricotage	320,157	10.8	281,895	3.9
Misr Silk Weaving Company	656,460	22.6	836,041	7.9
Usines Textiles al-Kahira	163,947	7.4	173,847	5.1
Alexandria Spinning and Weaving Company			670,202	0.0
Clothing and Equipment Company	200,000	15.8		
Cotton Spinning, Weaving and Dyeing Company, "Karnak"			495,635	3.1
al-Tawil Spinning and Weaving Company			923,205	22.1
Établissements Industriels Pour la Soie et le Coton	838,876*	13.9		
Fabrique Égyptienne des Textiles, "Ka-Bo"			359,000	19.5
Fayoum Textile Company	400,000*	2.5	415,156	4.2
Manufacture de Textiles Égyptiens, Matexa	169,301*	11.5	170,351	23.6
Nile Textile Company	548,414*	15.3	891,107	0.4
Orient Linen Industry	252,965*	6.2	292,967	7.0
Selected Textile Industries Association	328,830*	11.6	1,102,107	16.2
Société al-Chark Pour la Filature et le Tissage	425,000*	9.0	738,652	7.3
Société Arabe de Filature et de Tissage			761,529	26.2
Société Égyptienne de Filature et Tissage de Laine	915,964 –	13.0	771,614	14.5
Société Égyptienne de l'Industrie de Bonneterie, "La Bonneterie"			202,347	2.4
Société Égyptienne "Nouzha" de Filature et de Tissage			422,048	8.0
Société Égyptienne de Teinture et d'Appret			155,400	1.5
Société Industrielle des Fils et Textiles			1,770,000	11.8
Société Misr Pour la Rayonne			3,822,493	16.1
Société Nationale de Textile, "Memphis"			146,584	–5.6
Sociéte des Usines el-Shourbaghi Pour la Filature, le Tissage, et le Tricot			897,570	18.9
United Spinning and Weaving Company			317,503	16.6
Total	5,691,459		16,921,100	
Total excluding Misr firms	5,034,999		12,262,566	

* 1946–47 or 1947

Table 3.13
Percentage of Profits Paid out as Dividends, 1945–46 to 1955–56

	1945-46	46-47	47-48	48-49	49-50	50-51	51-52	52-53	53-54	54-55	55-56	Average
Filature	78	77	79	79	77	75	73	72	68	52	59	72
Misr Spinning and Weaving Company	82	82	82	82	81	84	82	83	83	77	86	82
Misr Fine Spinning and Weaving Company	56	60	60	60	60	64	65	64	64	73	66	63
Beida Dyers	96	105	100	99	89	110	100	100	42	46	54	86

Table 4.1
Egyptian and Foreign Capital Located in Joint Stock Companies Operating in Egypt, 1933-1948 (LE)

	Egyptian	Foreign	Total
Capitalization of companies founded before 1933—91% foreign, 9% Egyptian	6,006,635	60,733,751	66,740,386
Capitalization of new companies founded between 1933 and 1948— 21% foreign, 79% Egyptian	21,041,566	5,677,048	26,718,614
Increase in capitalization from 1933 to 1948 divided by same proportions, 21 to 79	19,260,632	5,213,378	24,476,000
Totals in 1948	46,308,823	71,624,177	128,030,000
Percentage	39%	61%	100%

Source: Majalla Ghurfa lil-Qahira, vol. 16, July and August, 1951, pp. 642-648.

Table 4.2
Nominal Capital, Reserves, Net Profits, and Dividends of Anglo-Egyptian Oil

	Nominal Capital	Depreciation Fund	Net Profits	Dividends on Common Stock	Exploration and General Reserve	Loans from Affiliates
	£	£	£	%	£	£
1911	676,000			none		
1912	1,000,000			none		
1913	1,250,000			none		
1914	1,350,000			none		
1915	1,350,000			none		
1916	1,350,000		342,156[a]	none		
1917	1,350,000		6,399	none		
1918	1,350,000	477,000		25[b]		
1919	1,808,000	543,363		20[c]		
1920	1,808,000	611,163		10		
1921	1,808,000	695,097		15		100,000
1922	1,808,000			12.5		100,000
1923	1,808,000	817,589		12.5		100,000
1924	1,808,000	874,002	176,609	10		100,000
1925	1,808,000	929,183	244,098	12.5		100,000
1926	1,808,000	983,800	245,136	12.5		100,000

... contd.

Table 4.2 continued

	Nominal Capital £	Depreciation Fund £	Net Profits £	Dividends on Common Stock %	Exploration and General Reserve £	Loans from Affiliates £
1927	1,808,000	1,036,280	328,000	17.5	100,000	
1928	1,808,000	1,079,000	424,266	22.5	30,548	
1929	1,808,000	1,153,000	449,806	22.5	100,000	
1930	1,808,000	1,245,361	345,662	17.5	100,000	
1931	1,808,000	1,318,780	161,709	17.5	100,000	
1932	1,808,000	1,393,278	194,399	10	100,000	
1933	1,808,000	1,486,061	220,910	10	150,000	
1934	1,808,000	1,575,249	225,929	10	200,000	
1935	1,808,000	1,671,159	212,342	10	200,000	
1936	1,808,000	1,760,442	233,937	12.5	197,688	
1937	1,808,000	1,854,522	234,992	12.5	160,569	
1938	1,808,000	1,963,662	188,993	12.5	108,431	
1939	1,808,000	2,101,183	323,941	12.5	108,803	
1940	1,808,000	2,260,724	236,254	12.5	100,000	
1941	1,808,000	2,433,780	241,180	12.5	100,000	
1942	1,808,000	2,645,592	186,225	12.5	100,000	
1943	1,808,000	2,881,433	159,154	12.5	100,000	
1944	1,808,000	2,037,455d	264,888	12.5	1,139,829d	
1945	1,808,000	2,273,813	251,462	12.5	1,300,000	
1946	1,808,000	2,545,315	520,525	12.5	1,650,000	
1947	1,808,000	2,811,807	544,877	12.5	2,000,000	750,000
1948	1,808,000	3,184,567	411,774	12.5	2,200,000	1,420,000
1949	1,808,000	4,182,020	385,818	12.5	2,400,000	1,635,386
1950	1,808,000	4,772,954	720,001	12.5	3,225,000	2,347,370
1951	1,808,000		207,310	12.5	3,800,000e	
1952	1,808,000		949,935	12.5	2,814,756	
1953	1,808,000		2,269,352	10	2,737,408	
1954	3,777,000f		1,800,179	12.5	4,607,428	
1955	3,777,000		2,519,263	10	4,671,641	

Sources: London Stock Exchange Official Yearbook, Stock Exchange Yearbook of Egypt, Investors Chronicle, and Egypt, Ministry of Finance, Department of Statistics, *Statistiques des Sociétés Anonymes.*

[a] Cumulative loss to 1916.
[b] B shares only.
[c] B shares only; company changed A shares into B shares; Egyptian government holds C shares.
[d] Accounting procedures changed for calculating depreciation fund and exploration and general reserve.
[e] A further change in accounting procedures, and no figures provided on the depreciation fund.
[f] The capitalization was doubled in 1954 by capitalizing £1,969,000 from the profits made in 1953.

Table 4.3
Profits and Reserve Funds of the Suez Canal Company,
1923-1955 (Fr. 000)

	Net Profits	Statutory Reserve	Extraordinary Reserve	Contingency Reserve	Pension Fund	Amortization Reserve
1923	285,691	40,519	60,000	5,990		
1924	373,339	40,519	80,000	5,877		
1925	486,340	40,519	100,000	5,621		
1926	619,810	40,519	120,000	5,520		
1927	659,794	40,519	140,000	5,482		
1928	716,298	200,000	61,449	25,431		
1929	742,740	200,000	61,449	25,431		
1930	714,484	200,000	61,449	23,991		
1931	564,795	200,000	11,449	11,828		
1932	494,462	200,000		9,667		
1933	547,602	200,000	25,000	23,744		
1934	546,748	200,000	50,000	33,933		
1935	585,622	200,000	85,000	30,172		
1936	627,940	230,000	85,000	29,658		
1937	852,716	280,000	85,000	39,148		
1938	928,097	305,000	100,000	50,980		
1939	554,540	305,000	100,000	50,980		
1940		305,000	100,000	50,980		
1941		305,000	100,000	50,980		
1942		305,000	100,000	67,000		
1943		305,000	100,000	152,000		
1944	774,567	305,000	100,000	829,000	101	1,491,714
1945	1,696,422	305,000	100,000	3,195,000	101	3,456,121
1946	4,439,334	305,000	800,000	3,195,000	96	4,551,149
1947	4,129,291	305,000	800,000	3,195,000	56,657	4,470,843
1948	13,827,615	430,000	2,000,000	3,195,000	184,197	12,310,764
1949	12,823,994	430,000	2,500,000	4,195,000	1,525,772	13,284,225
1950	16,162,185	430,000	5,000,000	4,495,000	1,644,351	14,747,924
1951	13,659,853	430,000	7,000,000	4,795,000	1,932,258	15,897,637
1952	13,651,097	430,000	9,000,000	4,995,000	1,152,621	17,104,223
1953	15,447,093	430,000	10,000,000	5,795,000	1,642,272	18,300,125
1954	15,593,811	430,000	11,000,000	6,395,000	2,033,839	19,243,774
1955	16,234,700	430,000	11,500,000	5,789,846	2,044,844	19,440,589

Sources: Egypt, Ministry of Finance, Department of Statistics, *Statistiques des Sociétés Anonymes; London Stock Exchange Official Yearbook;* and *Moody's Manual of Investments, American and Foreign: Public Utility Securities.*

Graph 4.1
Suez Canal Tonnage, 1946–1955

tonnage

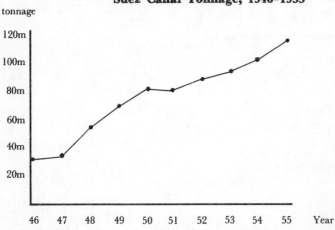

Suez Canal Company Receipts, Net Profits, and Dividends, 1946–1955

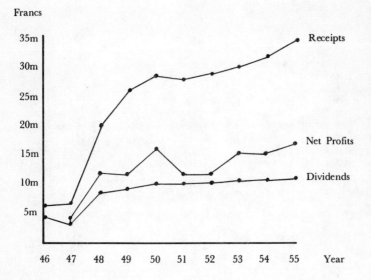

Sources: Farnie, *East and West of Suez* and *The Stock Exchange Official Yearbook*

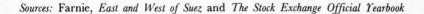

Notes

One: Introduction

[1]Bradford Dyers was absorbed by Viyella International, PLC; and Calico Printers by Tootal Textiles. I wish to thank Harry Leach of Tootal Textiles for allowing me access to the Calico records and to Jim Allison for permission to see the Bradford materials.

[2]Christopher Tugendhat, *The Multinationals* (London, 1971), p. x.

[3]For an emphasis on size, control, and oligopoly see Raymond Vernon, *Storm over the Multinationals: The Real Issues* (Cambridge, Massachusetts, 1977). Mira Wilkins offers a sparer definition in "Japanese Multinational Enterprise before 1914", scheduled for publication in the *Business History Review*. She suggests as multinationals those businesses which extend over borders and have regular employees in a foreign country Raymond Vernon in *Sovereignty at Bay: The Multinational Spread of U.S. Enterprise* (New York, 1971), p. 4, proposes a cutoff point of $100 million in total annual sales, but, of course, if one is trying to look at MNCs historically, such demarcation lines would be difficult to agree upon. Moreover, one of the arguments of this essay is that smaller firms, aspiring multinationals, must be taken account of when evaluating the impact of direct foreign investment on less-developed countries.

[4]Stephen Hymer, "The Multinational Corporation and the Law of Uneven Development", in *Economics and World Order from the 1970s to the 1990s*, edited by Jagdish N. Bhagwati (London, 1972), pp. 113-140 and D. K. Fieldhouse, *Unilever Overseas: The Anatomy of a Multinational, 1895-1965* (Standford, 1978).

[5]Raymond Vernon, *Sovereignty at Bay*, pp. 65-77.

[6]The most persuasive case study of terms of entry and their subsequent alteration is Theodore H. Moran, *Multinational Corporations and the Politics of Dependence: Copper in Chile* (Princeton, 1974).

[7]H. W. Singer, *The Strategy of International Development: Essays in the Economics of Backwardness*, edited by Alec Cairncross and Mohinder Pari (Plymouth, England, 1975); and Gunnar Myrdal, *Economic Theory and Under-Developed Regions* (London, 1957).

[8]Colin Leys, *Underdevelopment in Kenya: The Political Economy of Neo-Colonialism* (Berkeley, 1974), p. 138.

[9]For a useful discussion of these issues one should consult the review article of Kazimierz Z. Poznanski, "Technology Transfer: West-South Perspective", *World Politics*, vol. 37, no. 1, October, 1984, pp. 134-152.

[10]See the helpful review article of H. Jeffrey Leonard, "Multinational Corporations and Politics in Developing Countries", *World Politics*, vol. 32, no. 3, April, 1980, pp. 454-483.

[11]Steven Langdon, "Multinational Corporations, Taste Transfer, and Under Development: A Case Study from Kenya", *Review of the African Political Economy*, vol. 2, 1975, pp. 12-35.

[12]Maurice and Taya Zinkin, "Kenya—A Case Study of East African Industries, Ltd" (typescript, 1979), offer a spirited defense of Unilever's soap manufacturing industry in Kenya in reply to the charges made by Langdon.

[13]Egypt, Ministry of Finance, Statistical Department, *Annuaire Statistique*, 1914, pp. 295 and 297.

[14]M. P. S. Girard, "Mémoire sur l'agriculture, l'industrie, et le commerce de l'Égypte", *Description de l'Égypte, État moderne* (Paris, 1812), vol. 2, pt. 1, pp. 594-603.

[15]See the Egyptian trade statistics as compiled in Egypt, Ministry of Finance, Statistical Department, *Annuaire Statistique*, 1900+.

[16]Sidney H. Wells, "L'Industrie du tissage en Égypte", *Égypte contemporaine*, vol. 5, January, 1911, pp. 52-73 and "Note préliminaire sur l'industrie du tissage en Égypte", *Égypte contemporaine*, 1910, pp. 578-584.

[17]Egypt, *Rapport de la commission du commerce et de l'industrie* (Cairo, 1918), pp. 109-114.

[18]These reports may be found in the journal of the new Department of Commerce and Industry, *Sahifa al-tijara*, beginning with vol. 1, no. 1, October, 1924.

[19]*Égypte industrielle*, vol. 1, no. 5, 1926, pp. 74ff.

[20]Memorandum prepared for the UK mission by the Egyptian Department of Commerce and Industry, appendix to United Kingdom, *Report of the UK Trade Mission to Egypt*, February-March, 1931, pp. 51-56.

[21]Egypt, *Rapport de la commission du commerce et de l'industrie*, pp. 145-146.

[22]Ibid.

[23]*Bulletin commercial*, June 16, 1918, June 30, 1918, August 11, 1918, and July 13, 1919.

[24]*Sahifa al-tijara*, vol. 3, no. 3, April, 1927, pp. 1-6.

[25]Rene Maunier, "L'Exposition des industries égyptiennes", *Égypte contemporaine*, vol. 7, 1916, pp. 433-434.

[26]United Kingdom, Department of Overseas Trade, *Report on the Economic and Financial Situation in Egypt*, by E. H. Mulock, April, 1923, p. 25.

[27]These figures come from the memorandum prepared by the Egyptian Department of Commerce and Industry in the appendix to United Kingdom, Department of Overseas Trade, *Report of the UK Trade Mission to Egypt*, February-March, 1931, pp. 51-56.

[28]See Egypt, Ministry of Finance, Department of General Statistics, *Statistique des Sociétés Anonymes*, 1930-1933.

[29]See, in particular, R. Robson, *The Cotton Industry in Britain* (London, 1957) and Brian Toyne et al., *The Global Textile Industry* (London, 1984).

[30]See *Économiste égyptien*, June 26, 1927 and April 6, 1930 and *Égypte industrielle*, February, 1930, vol. 6, no. 2, pp. 47-56.

[31]See Tal'at Harb, "Taqrir 'an al-sina'a wa-l-tijara al-Almaniya", June 12, 1916 in Tal'at Harb, *Majmu'a khutab Muhammad Tal'at Harb* (Cairo, 1927), vol. 1, pp. 14ff.

[32]Tal'at Harb, *Majmu'a khutab*, vol. 1, pp. 96 and 109.

[33]Bank Misr, *al-Yubil al-dhahabi* (Cairo, 197?), p. 197.

[34]*Économiste égyptien*, May 6, 1928.

[35]*Sahifa al-tijara*, vol. 4, no. 2, January, 1928, pp. 21-22.

[36]*Informateur*, November 29, 1935.

[37]A. A. I. El-Gritly, "The Structure of Modern Industry in Egypt", *Égypte contemporaine*, nos. 241-242 (November-December, 1946) (entire issue), pp. 488-528.

Two: British Financial Intervention in Egyptian Textiles

[1]Douglas A. Farnie, "The Structure of the British Cotton Industry, 1846-1914", in Ako Okochi and Shin-Ichi Yonekawa, eds., *The Textile Industry and Its Business Climate* (Tokyo, 1982), p. 47 and Lars G. Sandberg, *Lancashire in Decline: A Study in Entrepreneurship, Technology, and International Trade* (Columbus, Ohio, 1974), p. 6.

[2]United Kingdom, House of Commons Sessional Papers, Committee on the Cotton Industry, *Report*, 1929-30, vol. 12, cmd. 3615, p. 5.

[3]Sandberg, *Lancashire in Decline*, p. 121 and United Kingdom, Committee on Industry and Trade, *Survey of Textile Industries* (London, 1928), being part III of a *Survey of Industries*.

[4]The hardest hit were those firms engaged in spinning coarse and medium yarns, mainly from American cotton. United Kingdom, Committee on Industry and Trade, *Survey of Textile Industries*, pp. 33-34.

[5]P. L. Payne, "The Emergence of the Large-Scale Company in Great Britain, 1890-1914", *The Economic History Review*, vol. 20, no. 3, December, 1967, pp. 519-542.

[6]Lennox B. Lee by A. Howe, typescript of article to be published in *The Dictionary of Business History*.

[7]Geoffrey Turnbull, *A History of the Calico Printing Industry of Great Britain* (Altincham, 1951), p. 325. One should also consult Henry W. Macrosty, *The Trust Management in British Industry: A Study of Business Organization* (London, 1907), pp. 117-180 and P. Lesley Cook, *Effects of Mergers: Six Studies* (London, 1958), pp. 133-214.

[8]John Clapham, *An Economic History of Modern Britain* (Cambridge, 1951), vol. 3, p. 229.

[9]United Kingdom, House of Commons Sessional Papers, The Monopolies and Restrictive Practices Commission, *Report on the Process of Calico Printing*, vol. 16, 1953-54, appendix 8, pp. 114-115, Statistics of CPA production.

[10]S. Yonekawa, "The Strategy and Structure of Cotton and Steel Enterprises in Britain, 1900-1938", in Keiichiro Nakagawa, ed., *Strategy and Structure of Big Business*

(Tokyo, 1974). Appendix I (pp. 250-251) gives dividends paid by Calico Printers, Bradford Dyers, and Bleachers. A slightly different picture emerges by considering profits rather than dividends, as a percentage of employed capital (equity plus reserves) (see table 2.4). The average profitability for Bleachers was 7.65%, Bradford 7.48%, and Calico 5.57%. This kind of calculation shows that Bleachers and Bradford had roughly the same profit rate. But whether we take dividend rate or profit rate Calico was less profitable than the other two. United Kingdom, Committee on Trade and Industry, *Survey of Textile Industries*, 1928, p. 42.

[11]United Kingdom, House of Commons Sessional Papers, The Monopolies and Restrictive Practices Commission, *Report on the Process of Calico Printing*, vol. 16, 1953-54, pp. 27-37.

[12]Ibid., p. 18.

[13]Ibid., pp. 114-115.

[14]Article by D. T. Jenkins on George Douglas for the *Dictionary of Business History*.

[15]See table in Yanekawa, "The Strategy and Structure of Cotton and Steel Enterprises in Britain, 1900-1939", in Nakagawa, ed., *Strategy and Structure of Big Business*, p. 241, and Macrosty, *The Trust Management in British Industry*, pp. 156ff.

[16]Ibid., pp. 250-251.

[17]Macrosty, *The Trust Management in British Industry*, pp. 141-142.

[18]United Kingdom, Committee on Industry and Trade, *Survey of Textile Industries*, 1928, pp. 33ff.

[19]Annual stockholders' reports, Calico Printers Association, 1929-1947.

[20]United Kingdom, House of Commons Sessional Papers, The Monopolies and Restrictive Practices Commission, *Report on the Process of Calico Printing*, vol. 16, 1953-54, pp. 114-115.

[21]Annual shareholders' reports, Bradford Dyers.

[22]Yonakawa, "The Strategy and Structure of Cotton and Steel Enterprises in Britain, 1900-1939", in Nakagawa, ed., *Strategy and Structure of Big Business*, pp. 242-243.

[23]See the Bradford Dyers' annual shareholders' report for 1932.

[24]Bradford Dyers, *Annual Report*, 1934.

[25]The best general account of the complex organization of the British cotton textile industry in the twentieth century can be found in R. Robson, *The Cotton Industry in Britain* (London, 1957). For the relationship of finishers and converters see especially pp. xiv and 85. Also United Kingdom, House of Commons Sessional Papers, Committee on the Cotton Industry, *Report*, 1929-30, vol. 12, p. 6.

[26]Minutes of the Board of CPA, vol. 14, February 16, 1932 and July 26, 1932 and vol. 15, January 10, 1933.

[27]Ibid., vol. 14, July 26, 1932.

[28]Ibid., vol. 15, January 10, 1933.

[29]Ibid., vol. 15, May 30, 1933.

[30]Ibid., vol. 16, August 29, 1933.

[31]Ibid., vol. 14, August 23, 1932. On Arno S. Pearse see his article, "Egyptian Cotton from the Point of View of the Spinning Industry", *Égypte contemporaine,* no. 127, March, 1931, pp. 388-389.

[32]Minutes of the Board of CPA, vol. 16, April 4, 1933.

[33]United Kingdom, Committee on Industry and Trade, *Survey of Textile Industries,* 1928, p. 77.

[34]Minutes of the Board of CPA, vol. 15, May 30, 1933.

[35]Ibid., vol. 16, August 29, 1933.

[36]Bolden to CPA, December 27, 1933, CPA M75/Secretariat Group file 102, Manchester Central Library.

[37]Minutes of the Board of CPA, vol. 16, September 12, 1933.

[38]N. G. McCulloch to Bolden, December 14, 1933, CPA 1975/Secretariat Group file 102, Manchester Central Library.

[39]Bolden to Secretary, January 1, 1934, CPA 1975/Secretariat Group file 102.

[40]Bolden to Secretary, January 17, 1934, CPA M75/Secretariat Group file 102.

[41]Bolden to Secretary, January 1, 1934, CPA M75/Secretariat Group file 102.

[42]For an introduction to this literature see Donald McCloskey and Roderick Floud, *The Economic History of Britain since 1700* (New York, 1981).

[43]See George Paish, "Great Britain's Capital Investment in Individual and Colonial Countries", *Journal of the Royal Statistical Society,* vol. 74 (1911), pp. 167-200.

[44]Bolden to Secretary, January 3, 1934, CPA M75/Secretariat Group file 102.

[45]Minutes of the Board of CPA, vol. 16, December 16, 1933.

[46]The agreement is discussed in Bolden to Secretary, January 3, 15, and 17, 1934 CPA, M75/Secretariat Group file 102.

[47]Bolden to Secretary, January 17, 1934, CPA M75/Secretariat Group file 102.

[48]Bolden to Secretary, January 15, 1934, CPA M75/Secretariat Group file 102.

[49]Minutes of the Board of CPA, vol. 18, August 20, 1935.

[50]Ibid., vol. 18, October 1, 1935.

[51]The modified agreement is to be found in CPA M75/Secretariat Group File 102.2, December 16, 1935.

[52]Figures from Egypt, Ministry of Finance, Department of General Statistics, *Statistique des Sociétés Anonymes,* 1940, pp. 223 and 254.

[53]See *Égypte industrielle,* vol. 9, No. 2, January 15, 1933, p. 24 and *Revue de'Égypte économique et financière,* December 14, 1940, pp. 8-9.

[54]These calculations were made from the reports of Egypt, Ministry of Finance, Department of General Statistics, *Statistique des Sociétés Anonymes,* 1930+.

[55]*Informateur,* April 28, 1933.

[56]*Informateur,* November 29, 1935.

[57]Minutes of the Management Board of BDA, December 16, 1937.

[58]Ibid.

[59]Selous to Department of Trade, May 14, 1937, Public Record Office, Foreign Office 371/20897 and Selous to Department of Trade, February 1, 1934, Public Record Office, 371/19985.

[60]Bank Misr, *al-Yubil al-dhahabi*, p. 198.

[61]Misr Spinning and Weaving Company, *Taqrir*, 1935–36.

[62]*Egyptian Gazette*, October 12 and 16, 1933.

[63]Ibid., October 9, 1933.

[64]See *al-Fallah al-iqtisadi*, vol. 1, no. 9, June 8, 1934, pp. 38–43; and *Informateur*, December 21, 1934 and January 25, 1935.

[65]Bank Misr, *Taqrir*, 1931, p. 17.

[66]Ibid., 1934, p. 16.

[67]Ibid., 1932, p. 17.

[68]Bank Misr, *al-Yubil al-dhahabi*, p. 191.

[69]Report by A. L. Anderson, Foreign Embarkations, January, 1937, BDA records and Minutes of Management Board, BDA, December 16, 1937.

[70]Minutes of Management Board, BDA, December 16, 1937 and Tal'at Harb, *Majmu'a khutab*, vol. 3, pp. 36ff.

[71]*Informateur*, December 21, 1934.

[72]*Economiste égyptien*, December 25, 1935.

[73]*Informateur*, January 25, 1935.

[74]S. Yonekawa, "The Strategy and Structure of Cotton and Steel Enterprises in Britain, 1900–39", in Nakagawa, ed., *Strategy and Structure of Big Business*, p. 243.

[75]Bradford Dyers Association, *Annual Report*, 1930.

[76]Ibid., 1938.

[77]*Investors Chronicle*, February 26, 1938.

[78]Bradford Dyers Association, *Annual Report*, 1938.

[79]Interview with G. W. Bird, May 14, 1984; Bradford Dyers, *Annual Report*, 1939; and Note on Position in Egypt, January 10, 1937, BDA records.

[80]Minutes of Managing Directors, BDA, October 14, 1935.

[81]Ibid., July 13, 1936.

[82]Ibid., January 2, 1936.

[83]Ibid., September 16, 1936.

[84]Ibid., September 16, and December 3, 1936.

[85]Ibid., December 3, 1936.

[86]Ibid., January 1, 1937.

[87]Keown-Boyd to H. R. Armitage, January 30, 1937, BDA records.

[88]Report by A. L. Anderson, Foreign Embarkation, January 1937, BDA records.

[89]Report entitled Necessity and Advantage of a Modern Spinning and Weaving Factory, n.d., BDA records.

[90]Position in Egypt, January 10, 1937, BDA records.

[91]A. Keown-Boyd to H. R. Armitage, May 12, 1937, BDA records.

[92]Position in Egypt, January 10, 1937, BDA records.

[93]Keown-Boyd to Armitage, May 12, 1937, BDA records.

[94]Armitage to Keown-Boyd, May 20, 1937, BDA records.

[95]Agreement, March 3, 1938, BDA records.

[96]Chronological Summary of the References to Egypt in the Executive Minutes, the board minutes, and the managing director's reports, August, 1938, BDA records.

[97]Interview with G. W. Bird, May 14, 1984 and typescript by G. W. Bird, Beida Dyers, S.A.E., May, 1984.

[98]*Majalla ghurfa al-Iskandariya*, vol. 1, no. 12, July, 1937, p. 10.

[99]Bank Misr, *Taqrir*, 1937, p. 10.

[100]André Eman, *L'Industrie du coton en Égypte: Étude d'économie politique* (Cairo, 1943), p. 77.

[101]See in particular Eric Davis, *Challenging Colonialism: Bank Misr and Egyptian Industrialization, 1920–1941* (Princeton, New Jersey: Princeton University Press, 1983), pp. 134–168.

[102]El-Gritly, "The Structure of Modern Industry in Egypt", *Égypte contemporaine*, 1947, p. 438.

[103]Eman, *L'Industrie du coton en Égypte*, pp. 59 and 170.

[104]Ibid., pp. 70ff.

[105]Ibid., p. 170.

[106]Ibid., p. 136.

[107]Ibid., p. 61.

Three: Textile Development 1940–1956

[1]National Bank of Egypt, *Economic Bulletin*, vol. 4, no. 2, 1951, p. 111.

[2]United Nations, Department of Economic and Social Affairs, *The Development of Manufacturing Industry in Egypt, Israel, and Turkey* (New York, 1958), p. 127.

[3]Bent Hansen and Girgis A. Marzouk, *Development and Economic Policy in the UAR (Egypt)* (Amsterdam, 1965), p. 114.

[4]SEIT, *Rapport*, 1945–46.

[5]Eman, *L'Industrie du coton en Égypte*, p. 15; Misr Spinning and Weaving Company, *Taqrir*, 1940, p. 6; *Taqrir*, 1944–45; and No. 565 Killearn to Foreign Office, March 7, 1945, Public Record Office, Foreign Office 371/45937.

[6]Egypt, Ministry of Finance and Economy, Statistical Department, *Industrial and Commercial Census*, 1947, pp. 6–8 and Egypt, Ministry of Finance, Department of Statistics and Census, *Annuaire Statistique*, 1944–45, pp. 394–395.

[7]United Nations, Department of Economic and Social Affairs, *The Development of Manufacturing Industry in Egypt, Israel, and Turkey*, p. 30.

[8]Egypt, Ministry of Finance and Economy, Statistical Department, *Industrial and Commercial Census*, 1947, pp. 398-399.

[9]Egypt, Ministry of Finance, Department of Statistics and Census, *Annuaire Statistique*, 1944-45, pp. 410-411.

[10]See report by Ashil Siqali in *Majalla ghurfa lil-Qahira*, vol. 14, December, 1949, pp. 1332-1342.

[11]*Majalla ghurfa al-Iskandariya*, vol. 5, December, 1940, p. 7.

[12]Egypt, *Annales de la Chambre des Députés*, 9th Legislature, 1st Session, February 14, 1945, pp. 3-5.

[13]Misr Spinning and Weaving Company, *Taqrir*, 1943-44, p. 6 and *Taqrir*, 1944, p. 6.

[14]Memorandum from the Commercial Counsellor to Headquarters, RAF, ME January 9, 1945, PRO FO 371/45937.

[15]*Stock Exchange Yearbook of Egypt*, 1943, p. 493 and 1947, p. 504 and Misr Spinning and Weaving Company, *Taqrir*, 1946, p. 3.

[16]No. 237, Killearn to Eden, February 12, 1945, PRO FO 371/45937.

[17]Letter from H. de G. Grantin, Director of British Northrup Loom Company to R. Tarfo, Egyptian Embassy in London, September 9, 1948, Egyptian National Archives, Ministry of Industry and Commerce, Department of Companies. By August, 1945, Platt Brothers alone had signed contracts to supply Egypt with 117,000 spindles. No. 47, Foreign Office to Cairo, November 10, 1945, PRO FO 371/45913.

[18]*Stock Exchange Yearbook of Egypt*, 1943, p. 501 and 1947, p. 509.

[19]Interview with G. W. Bird, May 14, 1984.

[20]Memorandum for the Foreign Compensation Commission Concerning SEIT, April 7, 1960, CPA archives.

[21]United Kingdom, Board of Trade, *Egypt*, 1947, p. 37.

[22]These data are assembled from a wide variety of sources: *Économiste égyptien*, *Revue de l'Égypte économique et financière*, and *Stock Exchange Yearbook of Egypt*.

[23]*Stock Exchange Yearbook of Egypt*, 1945, p. 640 and memorandum on Mr. François Tagher, June 6, 1955, Barclays Bank Archive Ml.3.

[24]*National Cyclopedia of American Biography*, vol. 48, pp. 12-13.

[25]*Économiste égyptien*, February 10, 1946 and February 17, 1946.

[26]Ibid., February 10, 1946.

[27]Ibid., January 18, 1948.

[28]*Stock Exchange Yearbook of Egypt*, 1957, pp. 423-428.

[29]Egypt, Ministry of Commerce and Industry, *Taqrir*, 1948, p. 54.

[30]"Compte rendu de l'exercice, 1948, Chambre de l'Industrie Égyptienne du Tricotage", *Égypte industrielle*, vol. 25, no. 5, May, 1949, p. 33.

[31]Hansen and Marzouk, *Development and Economic Policy in the UAR (Egypt)*, p. 115.

[32]United Nations, Department of Economic and Social Affairs, *The Development of Manufacturing Industry in Egypt*, p. 30.

[33]United Kingdom, Board of Trade, *Report on the Economic and Financial Situation of Egypt for 1955*, pp. 32ff.

[34]Misr Spinning and Weaving Company, *Taqrir*, 1948.

[35]*Économiste égyptien*, December 28, 1948.

[36]H. De Gandin, Director of British Northrop Loom Company to R. Tarfo, Egyptian Embassy in London, September 9, 1948, Egyptian National Archives, Ministry of Commerce and Industry, Department of Companies.

[37]A.G. Watson, Board of Trade, to Commercial Attaché, Egyptian Embassy, undated, Egyptian National Archives, Ministry of Commerce and Industry, Department of Companies.

[38]Ibrahim Abdel Koda Ibrahim, The Labor Problem in Industrialization in Egypt: A Case Study, Ph.D. thesis, Princeton University, p. 51.

[39] Hansen and Marzouk, *Development and Economic Policy in the UAR (Egypt)*, pp. 138ff and Robert Mabro, "Industrial Growth, Agricultural Under-Employment, and the Lewis Model. The Egyptian Case, 1937–1965", *Journal of Development Studies*, vol. 3, 1967, pp. 334ff.

[40]*al-Fajr al-jadid*, March 27, 1947.

[41]SEIT, *Rapport*, 1944–45; *Revue d'Égypte économique et financière*, August 10, 1946, p. 3; and *Économiste égyptien*, August 25, 1946.

[42]*Économiste égyptien*, September 15, 1946.

[43]SEIT, *Rapport*, 1954–55, pp. 7ff.

[44]*Majalla ghurfa lil-Qahira*, vol. 14, December 1949, pp. 1332–1342. On tariff protection one should consult Robert Mabro and Samir Radwan, *The Industrialization of Egypt, 1939–1973: Policy and Performance* (Oxford, 1976), pp. 50ff. They found the textile industry to be the second most heavily protected industry in Egypt.

[45]*Économiste égyptien*, May 9, 1948.

[46]Ibid., December 25, 1949.

[47]Ibid., May 15, 1949.

[48]Misr Spinning and Weaving Company, *Taqrir*, 1948–49.

[49]Eman, *L'Industrie du coton en Égypte*, p. 69.

[50]*Majalla ghurfa lil-Qahira*, vol. 14, December, 1949, pp. 1332–1342.

[51]*al-Ahram*, April 1, 1950.

[52]Calico Printers Association, *Annual Reports*.

[53]*The Statist*, vol. 154, p. 574.

[54]Calico Printers Association, *Annual Report*, 1945–46.

[55]Minutes of the board, March 6, 1945, CPA minutebooks, CPA records.

[56]No. 47 of 1950, Minutes of the board, December 12, 1950, vol. 40, CPA records.

[57]No. 7 of 1950, Minutes of the Board, February 7, 1950, vol. 38, CPA records.

[58]SEIT, *Rapport*, 1945-46.

[59]Extract from Minutes of the board meeting of SEIT, January 23, 1948 in CPA records M75, file 39(5), Manchester Central Library.

[60]No. 18 of 1951, Minutes of the board, August 14, 1951, vol. 40, CPA records.

[61]No. 28 of 1951, Minutes of the Board, December 4, 1951, vol. 40, CPA records.

[62]No. 13 of 1952, Minutes of the Board, May 20, 1952, CPA records.

[63]No. 7 of 1950, Minutes of the Board, February 7, 1950, vol. 38, CPA records.

[64]Procès-verbaux de la 73ème Réunion du Conseil d'Administration of SEIT, November 26, 1949, CPA records, M75, file 39(1), Manchester Central Library.

[65]No. 13 of 1952, Minutes of the Board, May 20, 1952, CPA records.

[66]Calico Printers Association, *Annual Reports*, 1953-54 and 1955-56.

[67]No. 7 of 1950, Minutes of the Board, December 4, 1951, CPA records.

[68]SEIT, *Rapport*, 1955-56, p. 12.

[69]No. 28 of 1951, Minutes of the Board, December 4, 1951, CPA records.

[70]No. 21 of 1951, Minutes of the Board, September 25, 1951, vol. 40, CPA records.

[71]No. 18 of 1951, Minutes of the Board, August 14, 1951, vol. 40, and No. 26 of 1951, Minutes of the Board, November 13, 1951, vol. 40, CPA records.

[72]Bradford Dyers Association, *Annual Reports*.

[73]Bradford Dyers Association, *Annual Report*, 1948.

[74]Ibid.

[75]Bradford Dyers Association, *Annual Report*, 1950.

[76]Bradford Dyers Association, *Annual Report*, 1951.

[77]Memorandum from Accountants Department, June 12, 1945, BDA records.

[78]Minutes of the Meeting of Directors, January 10, 1946, BDA Directors Minute Books, BDA records.

[79]Ibid.

[80]Interview with W. D. Fisher and J. H. E. Allison, April 17, 1984.

[81]Minutes of the Meeting of Directors, February 13, 1947, and July 21, 1949, BDA Directors Minute Books, BDA records.

[82]Minutes of the Meeting of Directors, December 20, 1948, BDA Directors Minute Books, BDA records.

[83]Minutes of the Meeting of the Directors, April 1, 1951, BDA Directors Minute Books, BDA records.

[84]Minutes of the Meeting of the Directors, December 17, 1953, BDA Directors Minute Books, BDA records.

[85]Bradford Dyers Association, *Annual Report*, 1953.

[86]Interview with W. D. Fisher and J. H. E. Allison, April 17, 1984.

[87]United Kingdom, Board of Trade, *Report on the Economic and Financial Situation of Egypt for 1955*, p. 33.

[88]Minutes of the Meeting of Directors, May 17 and May 31, 1956, BDA Directors Minute Books, BDA records.

[89]This large sum of money deposited with Bank Misr and the National Bank of Egypt was undoubtedly the proceeds from the sale of the Beida stock to the Misr group.

[90]Minutes of the Meeting of Directors, May 31, 1956, BDA Directors Minute Books, BDA records.

Four: Foreign Capital in Egypt in 1956

[1]A.E. Crouchley, *The Investment of Foreign Capital in Egyptian Companies and Public Debt* (Cairo, 1936).

[2]Egyptian Salt and Soda Company, Memo by W. R. Farmer, September 5, 1949, PRO FO 371/73542.

[3]Hossam Issa, *Capitalisme et Sociétés Anonymes en Égypte: Essai sur la Rapport entre Structure Sociale et Droit* (Paris, 1970) pp. 76–77.

[4]Gardener, Hunter, and Company to Capital Issues Committee, June 9, 1942, PRO T266/153 and Gardener, Hunter, and Company to Capital Issues Committee, April 6, 1943, PRO T266/153.

[5]Egyptian Salt and Soda Company, memo by W. R. Farmer, September 5, 1949, PRO 371/73542.

[6]Letter from Egyptian Salt and Soda Company to London Stock Exchange, March 13, 1958, attached to annual report of the company, 1955–56.

[7]*Egyptian Directory*, 1947 pp. 149–164.

[8]No. 789 R. Campbell to Bevin, July 3, 1946, enclosing memorandum presented to W. J. Johnson of the British Embassy by W. R. Farmer, June 21, 1946, PRO 371/53247.

[9]See, in particular, a series of articles written by Anis Mustafa Kamil on Jewish business influence in Egypt and published in *al-Ahram al-iqtisadi* in 1981 and 1982, especially the second in the series (March 30, 1981) on the Suares family.

[10]Francois Charles-Roux, "Le Capital Français en Égypte", *Égypte contemporaine* 8 (1911), p. 485; Gabriel Guémard, *Le Régime Hypothecaire Égyptien* (Aix, 1914), p. 63; and Crouchley, *The Investment of Foreign Capital in Egyptian Companies and Public Debt*, p. 34.

[11]Reffye, Consul in Cairo to Ministry of Foreign Affairs, December 10, 1906 and Reffye to de Valdrome, Chargé d'Affaires, Cairo, July 30, 1907, French Embassy Archives (FEA), Box 22.

[12]No. 220 Gaillard to Ministry of Foreign Affairs, December 28, 1931 FEA, Box 225.

[13]No. 20 French ambassador to Ministry of Foreign Affairs, January 24, 1934 FEA, Box 225.

[14]Vincenot to French Minister, Cairo, January 30, 1935, FEA, Box 225.

[15]*Egyptian Trade Index*, 1953, Alphabetical Section, p. 143.

[16]For the early history one should consult Jean Mazuel, *Le Sucre en Égypte: Étude de Géographie Historique et Économique* (Cairo, 1937).

[17]F. Charles-Roux, "Le Capital Français en Égypte", *Égypte contemporaine* 8 (1911), pp. 465–502; Cronier, Administrateur Delegué de la Raffinerie C. Say in Paris to Marquis de Reverseaux, May 13, 1893; No. 31 Reverseaux to Ministry of Foreign Affairs, June 21, 1893; and Consul in Paris to Hanotaux, Ministry of Foreign Affairs, May 23, 1895, FEA Box 232.

[18]Ernest Cassel bought up the sugarworks of the *Daira Sania* estates and then sold them to the Sugar Company in return for forty-eight payments of £56,000 each, spread over twenty-five years. *Journal du Caire*, October 29, 1902.

[19]No. 31 French Consul to M. Rouvier, September 7, 1905, FEA, Box 232.

[20]Reffye to Consul in Cairo, December 5, 1907, FEA, Box 232.

[21]Adhésion de l'Égypte à la convention de Bruxelles du Mars 5, 1902, April 1, 1908, FEA, Box 232 and Note by W. Brunyate, August, 1918, PRO FO 141/485.

[22]R. de Bercegal, Attaché Commercial à Monsieur le Ministre du Commerce et de l'Industrie, March 8, 1939, FEA, Box 233.

[23]R. de Bercegal, Attaché Commercial à Monsieur le Ministre du Commerce et de l'Industrie, January 10, 1939, FEA, Box 233.

[24]No. 1365, Mornard, Commercial Counselor in the French Embassy to Ministry of Foreign Affairs, May 19, 1956, FEA, Box 233.

[25]G. Hentenryk van-Kurgan, *Léopold II et les Groups Financiers Belges en Chine: La Politique Royale et ses Prolongements, 1895–1914* (Brussels, 1914), pp. 37–38.

[26]Ibid., p. 49.

[27]Albert Duchesne, "Héliopolis, Création d'Edouard Empain en Plein Désert: Une Page de la Présence Belge en Égypte", *Africa-Tervuen*, vol. 22, 1976, pp. 113–120 and l'Académie Royale des Sciences, des Lettres, et des Beaux-Arts de Belgique, *Biographie Nationale*, Supplement Tome VI (Brussels, 1967), pp. 266–270. When nationalized in 1960, the Cairo Electric Railway and Heliopolis Oases Company represented the largest Belgian holding in Egypt, at £15 million. The second largest was Banque Belge et Internationale en Égypte at £1 million. *The Times*, December 2, 1960.

[28]*Recueil Financier*, Paris, 1919.

[29]Julian Crossley and John Blándford, *The DCO Story: A History of Banking in Many Countries, 1925-71* (London, 1975), p. 1.

[30]Barclays Bank, Ltd. and Barclays Bank, DCO, *Annual Reports*, 1943–1944.

[31]*The Times*, December 31, 1956.

[32]Crossley and Blandford, *The DCO Story*, p. 127.

[33]Memorandum on The Suez Canal, August 2, 1956, Barclays Bank Archive M1.3.

[34]Hossani Issa, *Capitalisme et Sociétés Anonymes en Égypte,* pp. 219–20 and National Bank of Egypt, *The Economy of the United Arab Republic* (Cairo, 1963) pp. 18ff.

[35]*Annales de la Chambre des Deputés,* 7th Legislature, 3rd Session, March 11, 1940, pp. 258–260.

[36]Memo, National Bank of Egypt, April 19, 1939 by Hornsby; Hornsby to Cook, May 5, 1939; and A. D. Theodrakus to Hornsby, May 10, 1939 and July 17, 1939, Hornsby Papers at St. Antony's College, Oxford.

[37]*Majalla ghurfa al-Iskandariya,* vol. 3, no. 36, July, 1939, pp. 21–24.

[38]*Économiste égyptien,* June 18, 1950.

[39]National Bank of Egypt, *Economic Bulletin* vol. 3, 1950, pp. 80–85.

[40]National Bank of Egypt, *The Economy of the United Arab Republic,* pp. 18ff.

[41]The British American Tobacco Company, a conglomerate formed in 1902, began to acquire a number of Egyptian tobacco manufacturing and distribution companies, starting in 1920. By 1956 its affiliate in Egypt had a value of £17 million. The parent firm at that time had a nominal capital of £46,136,641, and the book value of the total assets of the parent and its many subsidiaries located all around the globe was no less than £323,576,836. On the Eastern Tobacco Company see Ducruet, *Capitaux Européens au Proche-Orient,* p. 323 and Nabil 'Abd al-Hamid Sayyid Ahmad, *al-Nashat al-iqtisadi lil-ajanib w-Atharuh fi-l-mujtama' al-Misri* (Cairo, 1982) pp. 204–206. The data on the British American tobacco Company are drawn from its *Stockholders Annual Report,* 1955–56.

A number of other multinationals established distributing firms in Egypt in the 1930s, most notably Imperial Chemical Industries, Ford Motor Company, General Motors, and Singer Sewing Machines. But Egypt had not yet become an important sales area for them.

[42]No. 970, High Commissioner to Foreign Office, September 12, 1919 and E. M. Dowson, Financial Adviser to Henry McMahon, July 11, 1921, PRO FO 141/426.

[43]*Investors Chronicle,* December 8, 1956 and memorandum, Egypt, no date but sometime in December, 1948, PRO FO 371/69242.

[44]*Financial Times,* August 6, 1950 and *Investors Chronicle,* June 10, 1950.

[45]*The Economist,* June 9, 1951.

[46]Caltex, a joint-venture marketing company of Standard Oil of California and Texaco, entered Egypt in 1937, but it failed to achieve a permanent place in the oil sector. Its share capital was limited to LE 80,000. No. 10, R. Campbell to Foreign Office, February 21, 1948, PRO FO 37/69184.

[47]These figures are taken from the various issues of Egypt, Ministry of Finance, Department of Statistics, *Annuaire Statistique.*

[48]Petroleum in Egypt, A Report Prepared for the Ambassador, November 29, 1949 USNA 883.6363/11-2949.

[49]E. M. Dowson, Financial Adviser to Henry McMahon, July 11, 1921, PRO FO 141/426.

[50]W. J. Jardine to Secretary of State, January 30, 1933, United States National Archives (USNA) 883.6363/39; Bert Fish to Secretary of State, April 21, 1936, USNA 883.6363/51; and No. 509, Campbell to Simon, May 27, 1933, Copy of

Egyptian Ministry of Finance Note on Kerosene and Petroleum Prices, May 23, 1933, PRO FO 371/17024.

[51] Petroleum in Egypt, A Report Prepared for the Ambassador, November 29, 1949, USNA 883.6363/11-2949.

[52] Memorandum, Egypt, no date, but December, 1948, PRO FO 371/69242. The Egyptian official in charge of oil matters, Dr. Abu Zayid, was a University of California graduate and petroleum engineer. He was said to be the only person in the government at that time (1949) with a petroleum background.

[53] D. H. Crofton, Ministry of Fuel and Power to Allen, Foreign Office, November 2, 1951, PRO FO 371/90172.

[54] Commercial Secretary to Africa Department, February 1, 1954, PRO FO 371/108539 JE 1532/1. These losses do not accord with the balance sheets of the company (see table 4.2), but they no doubt stem from the conflicts with the Egyptian government over the use of the stabilization fund.

[55] Memorandum to Haight from G. H. Stokes, December 29, 1948, Shell Archives, GHC/EG4/B2.

[56] Move of Control and Management to Egypt, October 25, 1949, Shell Archives GHC/EG4/B2.

[57] Howard to Haight, January 3, 1949, Shell Archives, GHC/EG4/B2.

[58] Chancery to Foreign Office, April 15, 1949, enclosing report on the conditions of work and amenities at Ras Gharib and Sudi oilfields by Alexander Gunn PRO FO 371/73641 and No. 86 Stevenson to Eden, April 3, 1952, enclosing report from the Egyptian Ministry of Social Affairs; Expert's Report on Minimum Wages, PRO FO 371/97078.

[59] Stevenson to Eden, February 12, 1954, PRO FO 371/108539 JE 1532/3.

[60] These concessions are described by the British Ambassador, Ralph Stevenson in JE1534/1 through JE1534/5 PRO FO 371/108543.

[61] L. M. Minford to T. E. Bromley, July 1, 1954, PRO FO 371/108539 JE 1532/16.

[62] Ibid.

[63] *Shubra*, May 6, 1937 and February 9, 1939.

[64] E. Papasian, *L'Égypte Économique et Financière* 1924-25, pp. 103ff.

[65] Heathcote Smith to Acting High Commissioner, January 29, 1934, PRO FO 141/499 on the Alexandria Water Company and its stormy relationship with the Alexandria Municipality. The campaign against these utility companies was led by 'Abd al-'Aziz Nazmi. See *Informateur*, March 17, 1933, *Revue d'Égypte économique et financière*, vol. 8, No. 80, February 11, 1934, and *Annales de la Chambre Des Députés*, 5th Legislature, 4th Session, April 24, 1934, pp. 175-176.

[66] Papasian, *L'Égypte Économique et Financiére*, 1924-25, pp. 286ff.

[67] The background to the law is covered in *Économiste égyptien*, January 29, 1939 and tel no. 83, Lampson to Foreign Office, January 27, 1939, PRO FO 371/23360. For the Law, see No. 878, Campbell to Bevin, October 22, 1947, PRO FO 371/63097.

[68] As an example see Moustapha el-Hefnawi, *Les problèmes contemporaines posés par le Canal de Suez* (Paris, 1951).

[69] The attitude of the Canal Company board to Hifnawi may be found in Wylie to Allen, September 6, 1951, PRO FO 371/90207.

[70] D. A. Farnie, *East and West of Suez: The Suez Canal in History, 1854-1956* (Oxford, 1969) pp. 607-608.

[71] Hankey to Clutton, August 25, 1948 and August 31, 1948, PRO FO 371/69241.

[72] No. 353, Campbell to Foreign Office, March 7, 1949, PRO FO 371/73601 and Farnie, *East and West of Suez*, pp. 671-672.

[73] No. 42, Campbell to Foreign Office, January 12, 1950, PRO FO 371/80325.

[74] D. R. Serpell to Allen, January 6, 1953, PRO FO 371/102887 and Serpell to Morris, Ministry of Treasury, February 19, 1953, PRO FO 371/102888.

[75] Note Complimentaire à la Note du 15 Juin, 1953, PRO FO 371/102892. The Company did in fact reduce tolls in 1951 and 1954, but not nearly as drastically as Serpell proposed. See Farnie, *East and West of Suez*, pp. 658 and 683.

[76] Wylie to Allen, December 23, 1952, PRO FO 371/102887.

[77] Wylie to Allen, July 8, 1953, PRO FO 371/102892. The Canal Company's transferable reserve was invested in 1953 as follows:

	Francs
French securities	
government stocks	588,000,000
debentures	216,000,000
stocks and shares	2,514,000,000
Foreign securities realizable in France	
shares	1,878,000,000
debentures	861,000,000
Foreign securities realizable abroad	
Belgian stocks and shares	512,000,000
British government loans,	
debentures, and shares	1,985,000,000
Egyptian government stocks	455,000,000
American shares	575,000,000
Miscellaneous	22,000,000
Total	9,626,000,000

[78] Wylie to Allen, April 2, 1953, PRO FO 371/102888.

[79] Wylie to Boothby, December 3, 1953, PRO FO 371/102892.

[80] *Middle East Economic Digest*, vol. 1, no. 16, June 28, 1957, p. 4.

[81] Ibid., vol. 2, no. 4, May 2, 1958, pp. 45-46.

[82] Ibid., vol. 2, no. 34, December 12, 1958, pp. 406-407.

[83] Ducruet, *Capitaux Européens au Proche-Orient*, p. 156.

[84] Unlike those of many of the other joint stock companies operating in Egypt, very few of the shares of the Canal Company had come into the possession of

Egyptians. In 1956 the shares were divided as follows:

France	360,139 shares	(45%)
British government	353,204 shares	(44.15%)
Switzerland	51,569 shares	(6.44%)
England	14,713 shares	(1.84%)
Egypt	1,609 shares	(0.20%)

Ducruet, *Capitaux Européens au Proche-Orient*, p. 144.

[85]United Kingdom, Board of Trade, *Report on Egypt*, 1955, pp. 38-39.

Bibliography

This study is based extensively on the uprinted records of two British textile firms: Bradford Dyers and Calico Printers. The bibliography will mention only those items cited in the notes. For a more comprehensive list of books on the twentieth-century Egyptian political economy, the reader should consult Robert L. Tignor, *State, Private Enterprise, and Economic Change in Egypt, 1918–1952* (Princeton, 1984).

Primary Sources: Archival

Bird, G. W., Beida Dyers, SAE, typescript. May, 1984.

Bradford Dyers Association, Minutes of the Management Board, Correspondence, and Reports laid before the Board.

Calico Printers Association, Correspondence in the Secretariat Group File, to be found in the Manchester Central Library.

Calico Printers Association, Minutes of the Board, soon to be deposited in the Manchester Central Library.

Egyptian National Archives, Ministry of Industry and Commerce, Department of Companies Records.

Foreign Office Correspondence (FO 141 and 371).

French Embassy Archives, Cairo.

Bertram Hornsby Papers, St. Antony's College, Oxford.

Shell Oil Archives, London.

United States National Archives, Correspondence to and from the American Embassy, Cairo.

Primary Sources: Newspapers, Journals, and Serial Publications

Africa-Tervuen
àl-Ahram
al-Ahram al-iqtisadi
Bulletin commercial
Économiste égyptien
Egypt. *Annales de la Chambre des Députés.*
Égypte contemporaine
Égypte industrielle
Egyptian Directory

Egyptian Gazette
al-Fajr al-jadid
al-Fallah al-iqtisadi
Financial Times.
Informateur
Investors Chronicle
London Stock Exchange Yearbook
Majalla ghurfa al-Iskandariya
Majalla ghurfa lil-Qahira
Middle East Economic Digest
National Bank of Egypt. *Economic Bulletin.*
Recueil Financier
Revue d'Égypte économique et financière
Sahifa al-tijara
Shubra
The Statist
Stock Exchange Yearbook of Egypt
The Times

Primary Sources: Books and Articles

Bank Misr. *Taqrir.*
Bank Misr. *al-Yubil al-dhahabi.* Cairo, 197?.
Barclays Bank. *Annual Reports.*
Barclays Bank, DCO. *Annual Reports.*
Bradford Dyers Association. *Annual Reports.*
British American Tobacco Company. *Annual Reports.*
Calico Printers Association. *Annual Reports.*
Egypt. *Rapport de la Commission du Commerce et de l'Industrie.* Cairo, 1918.
Egypt, Ministry of Finance, Department of General Statistics. *Statistiques des Sociétés Anonymes.*
Egypt, Ministry of Finance, Statistical Department. *Annuaire Statistique.*
Egypt, Ministry of Finance and Economy, Statistical Department. *Industrial and Commercial Census,* 1947.
Girard, M. P. S. "Mémoire sur l'Agriculture, l'Industrie, et le Commerce de l'Égypte", *Description de l'Égypte, État Moderne,* Vol. 2, Part 1, pp. 594–603. Paris 1812.
Harb, Tal'at. *Majmu'a Khutab Muhammad Tal'at Harb,* 3 Vols. Cairo, 1927+
Misr Spinning and Weaving Company. *Taqrir.*
National Cyclopedia of American Biography
Nakagawa, Keiichiro, ed. *Strategy and Structure of Big Business.* Tokyo, 1974.
Papasian, E. *L'Égypte Économique et Financière.* Cairo, 1924–25.
Société Égyptienne des Industries Textiles. *Rapports.*
United Kingdom. *Report of the United Kingdom Mission to Egypt.* February–March, 1931.
United Kingdom. Board of Trade. *Egypt.* 1947.
United Kingdom. Board of Trade. *Report on the Economic and Financial Situation of Egypt for 1955.*

United Kingdom. Committee on Industry and Trade. *Survey of Textile Industries*, Part 3. London, 1928.

United Kingdom. Department of Trade. *Report on the Economic and Financial Situation in Egypt*, E. H. Mulock. April, 1923.

United Kingdom, House of Commons Sessional Papers, Committee on the Cotton Industry. *Report*, 1929–30, Vol. 12, cmd. 3615.

United Kingdom, House of Commons Sessional Papers, The Monopolies and Restrictive Practices Commission. *Report on the Process of Calico Printing*, Vol. 16, 1953–54.

United Nations, Department of Economic and Social Affairs. *The Development of Manufacturing Industry in Egypt, Israel, and Turkey*. New York, 1958.

Secondary Sources

Ahmad, Nabil 'Abd al-Hamid Sayyid. *al-Nashat al-iqtisadi lil-ajanib w-atharuh fi-l-mujtama' al-Misri*. Cairo, 1982.

Clapham, John. *An Economic History of Modern Britain*, Vol. 3. Cambridge, 1951.

Cook, P. Lesley. *Effects of Mergers: Six Studies*. London, 1958.

Crossley, Julian, and John Blandford. *The DCO Story: A History of Banking in Many Countries*. London, 1975.

Crouchley, A. E. *The Investment of Foreign Capital in Egyptian Companies and Public Debt*. Cairo, 1936.

Davis, Eric. *Challenging Colonialism: Bank Misr and Egyptian Industrialization, 1920–1941*. Princeton, 1983.

Dictionary of Business History

Ducruet, Jean. *Capitaux Européens au Proche Orient*. Paris, 1964.

Eman, André. *L'Industrie du Coton en Égypte: Étude d'Économie Politique*. Cairo, 1943.

Farnie, D. A. *East and West of Suez: The Suez Canal in History, 1854–1956*. Oxford, 1969.

Fieldhouse, D. K. *Unilever Overseas: The Anatomy of a Multinational, 1895–1965*. Stanford, 1978.

Guemard, Gabriel. *Le Régime Hypothécaire Égyptien*. Aix. 1914.

Hansen, Bent, and Girgis A. Marzouk. *Development and Economic Policy in the UAR (Egypt)*. Amsterdam, 1965.

Hymer, Stephen. "The Multinational Corporation and the Law of Uneven Development", in *Economics and World Order from the 1970s to the 1990s*, ed. by Jagdish N. Bhagwati. London, 1972.

Ibrahim, Ibrahim Abdel Koda. The Labor Problem in Industrialization in Egypt: A Case Study. Ph.D. Thesis, Princeton University.

Issa, Hossam. *Capitalisme et Sociétés Anonymes en Égypte: Essai sur la Rapport entre Structure Sociale et Droit*. Paris, 1970.

Langdon, Steven. "Multinational Corporations, Taste Transfer, and Underdevelopment: A Case Study from Kenya", *Review of the African Political Economy*, Vol. 2 (1975), pp. 12–35.

Leonard, H. Jeffrey. "Multinational Corporations and Politics in Developing Countries", *World Politics*, Vol. 32, No. 3 (April, 1980), pp. 454–483.

Leys, Colin. *Underdevelopment in Kenya: The Political Economy of Neo-Colonialism*. Berkeley, 1974.

Mabro, Robert. "Industrial Growth, Agricultural Under-Employment, and the Lewis Model. The Egyptian Case, 1937–1965", *Journal of Development Studies*, Vol. 3 (1967).

Mabro, Robert, and Samir Radwan. *The Industrialization of Egypt, 1939–1973: Policy and Performance*. Oxford, 1976.

Macrosty, Henry W. *The Trust Management in British Industry: A Study of Business Organization*. London, 1907.

Mazuel, Jean. *Le Sucre en Égypte: Étude de Géographie Historique et Économique*. Cairo, 1937.

McCloskey, Donald, and Roderick Floud. *The Economic History of Britain since 1700*. New York, 1981.

Moran, Theodore H. *Multinational Corporations and the Politics of Dependence: Copper in Chile*. Princeton, 1974.

Myrdal, Gunnar. *Economic Theory and Under-Developed Regions*. London, 1957.

National Bank of Egypt, *The Economy of the United Arab Republic*. Cairo, 1963.

Okochi, Akio, and Shin-Ichi Yonekawa, eds., *The Textile Industry and Its Business Climate*. Tokyo, 1982.

Paish, George. "Great Britain's Capital Investment in Individual and Colonial Countries", *Journal of the Royal Statistical Society*, Vol. 74 (1911), pp. 167–200.

Payne, P. L. "The Emergence of the Large-Scale Company in Great Britain, 1890–1914", *Economic History Review*, Vol. 20, No. 3 (December, 1967), pp. 519–542.

Poznanski, Kazimierz Z. "Technology Transfer: West-South Perspectives", *World Politics*, Vol. 37, No. 1 (October, 1984), pp. 134–152.

Robson, R. *The Cotton Industry in Britain*. London, 1957.

Sandberg, Lars. *Lancashire in Decline: A Study in Entrepreneurship, Technology, and International Trade*. Columbus, Ohio, 1974.

Singer, H. W. *The Strategy of International Development: Essays in the Economics of Backwardness*, ed. by Alec Cairncross and Mohinder Pari. Plymouth, England, 1975.

Toyne, Brian, et al. *The Global Textile Industry*. London, 1984.

Tugendhat, Christopher. *The Multinationals*. London, 1971.

Turnbull, Geoffrey. *A History of the Calico Printing Industry of Great Britain*. Altincham, 1951.

van-Kurgan, G. Hentenryk. *Léopold II et les Groups Financiers Belges en Chine: La Politique Royale et ses Prolongements, 1895–1914*. Brussels, 1914.

Vernon, Raymond. *Sovereignty at Bay: The Multinational Spread of United States Enterprise*. New York, 1971.

Storm over the Multinationals: The Real Issues. Cambridge, 1977.

Index

Produced by the Printshop
of
the American University in Cairo Press